Praise for *Buddha*

Buddha's Flower–Newton's Apple portrays a strong and original mind deeply engaged with a number of exacting traditions for achieving enlightenment. It is also a compelling memoir, filled with incident, incisive portraits and unusual relationships. With candor and vivid recall, the author describes the experience of being both student and teacher in the quest to reach the state of "non-dual awareness" in Zen Buddhism and, to a lesser extent, by investigating other teachings. She is very gifted at getting to the core of various (somewhat) esoteric beliefs and theories of mind, cognition and sensation, providing a reader with flashes of insight and comprehension. These things are very difficult to write about and the author uses analytic abstraction and concrete specificity to great effect.

It is an original, honest, readable and very moving account of a lifelong search to understand her own mind (a remarkable one!) and its potential for transcendence.

—**Elizabeth Diefendorf**
Former Chief Librarian, General Research
Division, New York Public Library

Standing at the top of the proverbial 100 step ladder, Dagmar Apel takes one more step and in doing so points directly and courageously to the moon of non-dual awareness. She persistently investigates and poses profoundly significant questions to those sincerely on the path of Zen. What is this non-dual awareness? What is it for? Is it the thing itself or is it only one more signpost on the path of Zen? Her honesty and humor richly bring out the humanity of being fully in this moment where no thing really exists except what we make of it.

—**Jo Potter**
Dharma Master (Korean Zen Buddhism)

BUDDHA'S FLOWER NEWTON'S APPLE

One Person's Exploration of Enlightenment
in a Material World

Dagmar Apel

RHENUS PRESS

Published by Rhenus Press, Bronxville, NY

© 2016 Dagmar Apel

ISBN: 978-0-69276-231-8

ON THE COVER:
Detail from *Buddha* © 2016 Bob Shamis
Detail from *Sir Isaac Newton*, 1702, oil on canvas, by Gottfried Kneller (1646–1723)

Book and cover design by Gregory Wakabayashi

For more informaton about author please visit: www.dagmarapel.com

Contents

für dich, meine Mutter

Acknowledgments

W RITING ABOUT A SUBJECT AS COMPLEX AND UNCOMMON as "enlightenment" is a difficult task, but doing so in a non-native language proved almost impossible. I would never have succeeded if not for the immeasurable generosity of my husband Bob Shamis. I cannot express my gratitude profoundly and deeply enough for his patience in reading and correcting every draft and repeated revisions and for his support in every step of this enterprise. I would like to thank my readers Julia Ballerini, Geta Carlson, Sally Fox, Sue Haven, and Diana Reese for their interesting and intelligent comments on the several versions of my manuscript and for their heartfelt encouragement. I also want to thank my editor, Neil Mann, for his enthusiasm and the unfailing and refined sense of language that he brought to this unusual subject and text. Many conversations preceded and even sometimes initiated the topics I later felt the need to investigate. I thank the late Toni Packer, Andrea Bold, Isaac Gewirtz, Waltraud Irland, Jan Sendzimir, and the many friends who shared their interest in this subject matter. And last, but not least, I need to give my heartfelt thanks to Kristin Griffith who, with her generous gift, made this adventure possible.

Preface

WHAT IS ENLIGHTENMENT? HOW CAN IT BE DESCRIBED without using the terms of religion and tradition? Can you express an experience that resists all category and concepts of definition? Can an enlightened state carry over into normal life or is it inevitably a special state reserved for retreat from the world? Is enlightenment a spiritual state? Does it have any moral effect? Is an enlightened person a better person? How does the nature of reality appear to someone who is enlightened?

Enlightenment is a loaded word, both vague and precise. For many people the term enlightenment carries a particular significance. It may mean a specific behavior, an exclusive knowledge, an overall understanding of the human condition of life and death, or a state of true happiness and peace. For many Buddhists, enlightenment means all of these, together with the possibility of attaining such a goal over many lifetimes or waking up to it within one's present life.

A word that is readily understandable—like "enlightenment"—is liable to be misleading, while special terms—like "*kensho*" or "non-dual awareness"—are initially barriers to understanding and only acquire significance with familiarity. Most of the terms find meaning within a very specific religious framework, even if, ultimately, they do not depend on the religion itself. The understanding of this state of consciousness that I finally arrived at is very different from the concept I originally encountered and assimilated when I first began studying Zen Buddhism.

I heard about this prospect of knowing the true nature of the universe and everlasting happiness when I was in my late twenties. After seven years of arduous Zen training I finally experienced *kensho*, "a glimpse of enlightenment," as the usual translation carefully words it. This book is my account of some forty years spent trying to cultivate, integrate, and make sense of this condition, often called non-dual awareness.

It is a paradox for me that, after forty years of experiencing the vanishing of self or of dissolving the division between self and world, the best way to address the questions and explain my thoughts seems to be through telling my own life and my very personal findings. I lay no claim to authority beyond my own experience and my own understanding. This narrative is not meant as a scholarly investigation into philosophical or scientific findings. My interest and intent is not to proclaim some new truth or discount other people's personal creeds, but rather to initiate a dialogue and provide the basis for further exchange. For those with an open mind and an interest in the nature of consciousness, in how we perceive reality, and in how the physical world of Newton relates to the metaphysical realm of Buddha, I want to share one person's journey.

Chapter 1

The Promise

I WAS NOT HAPPY. THE CALL HAD FINALLY COME. WE WERE TO FLY to Japan as part of the music program for the German pavilion at the World's Fair in Osaka. It was 1970; I was twenty-seven years old and the first soprano of a vocal ensemble in hot demand for performances of "Stimmung," a piece by the contemporary composer Karlheinz Stockhausen that is celebrated as one of the first to use and amplify the sounds of overtones produced while singing. Yet I didn't want to spend time separated from my lover and I wanted to keep looking at the overflowing Rhine rushing through the old parts of Cologne. At this point, my interest in Japanese culture was mostly focused on "hot fudge sundaes," an ice-cream dish I had discovered when living in the U.S. a few years earlier. Knowing that Japan had been occupied by American soldiers, I was sure I would be able to indulge in it again. Instead, I found a fastidious, utterly alien culture and a completely new outlook on life.

It was March, wet and cold, when we arrived. In the suburbs of Osaka, our mezzo-soprano Helga and I found a small apartment, well equipped with the grassy scent of fresh tatami but nothing else. No heat and no hot water either. The bathtub had to be filled with water first and then warmed by a gas heater that could only be turned on from the outside. In 1970 many people would still go to public baths wearing cotton *yukatas*, the typical Japanese house robes. We set out to buy an electric heater, two chairs, and a little table.

I discovered that I didn't care much for the famous tea ceremony but loved Noh plays. The slow tempo and peculiar mode of the unfolding drama in Noh and the unfamiliar music held me spellbound. I preferred it even to the Bunraku, the famous puppet theater of Osaka. But the real surprise came not in the environment but in myself, when I came across a book about Zen meditation.

In the early seventies in Japan it was not easy to find reading material in a European language. What we had were books that my roommate had gotten from her journalist husband in order to gain some understanding of this very foreign culture, which we had landed in with little preparation. One of those books had little to do with Japan itself, but was actually one of the first modern books for westerners with practical information about Zen Buddhism. It was called *The Three Pillars of Zen*. When I started to read this book, I had no intention of studying Buddhism. I was just curious to learn more about Japan and Buddhist culture. Instead, I read that my mind was a chattering monkey and I needed to cultivate an inner silence in order to become enlightened. To do this properly, you were to start counting your breaths and not be diverted from this task. I was enthralled. That was all? It couldn't be that difficult.

Reading further, I gathered, somewhat to my puzzlement, that human nature and all existence are intrinsically whole and flawless—in a word, perfect. I just needed to awaken to this fact announced by the Buddha. This very discovery was called enlightenment—so I understood. What makes us suffer is our sense of being a separate self that gives rise to likes and dislikes—in short, the "ego." I certainly wanted to stop suffering—who wouldn't?

Except in my early childhood, I have felt no affinities with religion. Zen teaching, as I learned from reading this book, did not ask you to believe in either the Buddha or anything else it expounded, but urged you to find this "Truth" through your own experience. I liked this attitude. I had no interest in anything that sounded remotely "spiritual." I also found the implication that my experience of the world and myself was an illusion very attractive.

Before reading *The Three Pillars of Zen*, I had just finished some short stories by Jorge Luis Borges that I had taken along and was deeply baffled by the conundrum of whether opposing concepts like "hot" and "cold" cancel each other out or are necessary to each other. Without loud would there be no quiet? Without hard, no soft? If there was no hard and no soft, then what? Is what I perceive as bright or dark not real? It truly nagged me, and I believe this quandary brought me closer to considering that perhaps even this very important person, known as "myself," might not be quite as real as it seemed.

Another reason why I was so fascinated by the ideas Zen had implanted in my mind was that, although I am very impulsive and quick to make decisions, even as a child I would often stop to contemplate notions that other people didn't seem to bother about. Why can we count and animals can't? Why do we have no fur? Is there life anywhere besides Earth? Even before the first satellite went up, I had drawn charts of the range of the various rockets that were shot into the atmosphere surrounding the Earth. I was called "the thinker" in school because I had early on developed a deep, vertical crease between my eyebrows, much to my displeasure once I became aware of it. Nevertheless I always was drawn to the "why" explanations rather than to the "how" descriptions.

The Three Pillars of Zen gave me precise answers. The vision I obtained was decisive: If enlightenment could be attained, a global "win-win" situation would arise. Not only would I be eternally happy but the whole universe would heal. I was also given to understand that *zazen*, as meditation was called in Zen, was not to be confused with general meditation practice since, through doing *zazen*, "the mind is freed of all thought forms…and brought to a state of absolute emptiness, from which alone it may one day perceive its own true nature, or the nature of the universe."[1] Further, the practice of *zazen* rested solely on faith in an existence that is "intrinsically whole, flawless and omnipotent."

I will always wonder what would have happened if I had just practiced quiet non-judgmental observation of my breathing and the flow of my thoughts and emotions without emphasis on enlightenment, as you are advised in other methods of meditation. But this was not to be, because I had found "The Book"—as I capitalized it in my mind—which considered counting the breath simply a preliminary exercise on the way towards much "higher" goals. Therefore, in my typically enthusiastic manner, I fully embraced the idea of mastering awareness of my breath as a means to calm my mind and a first step to enlightenment.

After a few months in Osaka, I had learned to count in Japanese and direct the cab drivers towards our train station, and the weather had not only gotten hot, but it felt as if the air was dripping wet. People often came into the big, round German exposition building where we sang less to listen to the strange-sounding, modern music than to cool off, feed their kids, or simply snore away. So, after a long day of performing, I was standing in line for a cab, looking over an ocean of black-haired heads in front of me, feeling impatient and bored as I waited to get home. Silently, but tenaciously, I started counting my breaths. One. In – out. Two. In – out. Three. In – out. Four…and so on, up to ten and then again from one. When I lost count, I started over. This strange exercise was somehow working. I was amazed that something so simple could, even if only for a time, alleviate my fidgeting and my irritation about the endless wait.

Even though I was in Japan for eight months, I never really made the connection with any Zen activities going on there. Certainly, I immediately felt very drawn to the peaceful sturdiness of the square and firm sitting of the Buddhas, and to the erect posture but fluid gestures in the depictions of the Bodhisattva Avalokiteshwara (better known by the Chinese name Kuan Yin), but the idea of trying to seek out any form of Buddhist instruction never arose. I was completely satisfied with what I had learned through Kapleau's book and found the instructions clear. Knowing how much the "preliminary" exercise of counting my breath had already helped me stay calm and composed, I was completely convinced that all other promises would come true if only I poured enough diligence and perseverance into my practice. I started to inquire about the author of the book in order to find out how I could make this happen, eventually learning that he was no longer in Japan but had opened a Zen center in the northeastern United States.

Back in Cologne, my acquired taste for silent sitting grew more intense. My streetcar stop soon became the focus for my meditative diversion from boredom. Handily situated at the stop was a vending machine displaying all kind of sweets that always lured me as a reward for waiting. But, if I could hold out long enough, counting my breath, the streetcar would come without my having given in to temptation.

As a professional singer, and having been brought up playing the violin, I was used to the concept of practicing. In fact, as a singer, I had also learned that, just because practice rooms where easily available at eight in the morning, it did not mean that my voice would be as willing to run scales as my hands were on the violin at this time of day. I had to recognize and respect my own limits. In this regard I had a long way to go, as I was to discover rather painfully over many years. Since I didn't expect to find a group of people meeting somewhere and doing, well, nothing, I sat almost every evening for an hour by myself. Over the course of a year, I came to have considerably more success at slowing down my mental activity than in the beginning, but I also started identifying myself as a very special person who was on her way to eternal freedom, if not immortality. One evening, when I was lying down on my bed instead of sitting and quieting my mind—in Zen one never closes eyes when meditating—I heard some kind of roaring and felt as if I were sliding into something like a long tunnel with a bright opening in the end. I had read about experiences like this and therefore quite expected to die and awaken into nirvana.

Of course, today I know that I was never in any danger of drifting into anything like a faint or any other form of oblivion, but this was one of many experiences that intensified my awareness that there is a need to look at how meditation is supported and a need for instruction. Focusing the energy into the center of the body, an aspect of traditional Zen training, with an emphasis on keeping an unperturbed state of mind while in pain and distress, can be enormously helpful, but it can also get in the way of being in touch with deeper needs of the body-mind. It certainly did nothing to help me learn how to relax and calm my nervous system. Why would I even consider such a thing? I was out to conquer my ego and find the absolute solution to suffering.

Chapter 2

First Contact

I FINALLY FOUND OUT THAT PHILIP KAPLEAU, THE AUTHOR OF *The Three Pillars of Zen* was heading a Zen center in the city of Rochester, in upstate New York. Strangely enough, I had lived in nearby Buffalo for a few months in 1965 with my first husband (a composer, who had had a fellowship at the State University), and knowledge of the area had not created any great desire to live there again. But my reluctance was countered by the need to deepen my understanding of *zazen*.

After Collegium Vocale's appearance at the Osaka World Expo, we got more and more offers to perform Stockhausen and other contemporary pieces, together with our repertoire of Renaissance music. We started to travel all over the world, partly facilitated by the German cultural organization called the Goethe Institut. In December 1971, our ensemble toured North America together with Maurice Bejart's "Ballet of the 20th Century," finishing with a performance in the Canadian city of Ottawa. I had already decided to stay on and cross the border to visit the Zen Center in Rochester. Through a friend, I managed to make contact with Philip Kapleau's wife, Delancy, who agreed to meet me at the hotel where I was staying for the concert in Ottawa. It soon became clear that the couple had separated a while earlier, since Delancy, extremely charming and persuasive, encouraged me to take that first step and participate in the Center's activities, while also making it very clear that she hardly ever went near it. She had turned towards a Hindu form of spiritual discipline, if I remember correctly, and was no longer interested in Zen.

It was all a bit confusing and I anxiously looked forward to meeting Toni Packer, a disciple of Kapleau's, who I had been put into contact with through a German member of the Rochester Zen Center. German by birth, Toni lived with her husband and son in Tonawanda, a suburb of Buffalo, about one and a half hours away from Rochester. We'd arranged that I would visit her at home and we would then drive together to Rochester where I would meet Kapleau for the first time.

Toni, a vivacious woman in her early forties, greeted me warmly. The Packers took me for a walk along the banks of the river, and we watched the famous Niagara Falls crash down into the huge abyss. But what was even more impressive for me back then was the basement of the Packers' house. It was clean and comfortable, complete with "sitting" (*zazen*) room, generously furnished with cushions and—most important—housed a big washing machine and a dryer, wonders to me at the time, new and truly astonishing. (In the coming years, every time I visited the Center via Buffalo, I would always arrive with my suitcase full of dirty laundry.) That first time, Toni made sure that there were lots of meals prepared for her family while she was away, and then off we went to meet my fate in Rochester.

The Zen Center at 7 Arnold Park was a beautiful mansion on a quiet street, lined with old trees, and it is still there. As we entered, my first impressions were of polished wood all around, a quiet atmosphere, and a friendly welcome. We arrived just in time for the evening sitting, and I was shown to a place in a smallish room with mats and round cushions (the "sub *zendo*" or smaller sitting hall, as I later learned).[2] So I sat down, tucked my legs under me, as best I could, and did what I had taught myself to do over the previous year. The rhythm of wooden clappers and the sound of bells starting a round of sitting were new and somewhat distracting. I was also confused by the slow and ritualistic walking that took place between the rounds until I remembered having read about it as a form of *zazen*. So I diligently counted my breaths and tried to stick to this counting. Suddenly, and after what seemed just a short time, I felt rudely interrupted by a face bending down over me. I looked up, somewhat startled, and met a smile with kind eyes. It was "the *roshi*," as Kapleau was called in his function as Zen teacher; he had not seen me before and seemed pleased with my reaction. He reassured me to carry on and continued his round.

I was happy but also preoccupied with learning the meaning of the different sounds guiding *zazen* activities and with participating in chanting the texts, some of which were already translated into English and seemed quite mystical and awe-inspiring. One was the Heart Sutra, which states that there is "no eye, ear, nose, tongue, body, mind..."[3] This seemed like a rather doleful outlook but was also quite intriguing, given the reward it promised of eternal happiness or such. Back then, of course, I had no inkling that one day I would be a teacher and make use of these very lines with a different spin. Even today, while not remembering much of the chants or other Buddhist writings, I feel this special sutra skillfully describes a state of consciousness that is certainly not "eternal happiness" but an aspect of a specific awareness that has become a significant part of my life. But, until all this was understood, I thought in terms of effort and reward in pursuing my "True Nature."

Chapter 3

The Training

AFTER MY INITIAL VISIT AND INTRODUCTION, I LEFT THE Center and Toni for Europe, already planning to return to the U.S. I was glowing with a sense of destiny and eagerness to come back and get enlightened. I also became a vegetarian. I seemed to thrive on empty walls, rigid posture, and most of all the rightness of doing this. What more special thing on earth could I do but find out who and what I truly was? Why wouldn't everybody want to do that?

Whenever my concert schedule allowed, I returned to the Center. I slowly caught on to the rules of conduct and the philosophy behind them. You were not to engage in conversation unless it connected to the business at hand and you were to attend fully to the given task. Zen aimed to integrate formal meditation into daily living. This was also evident in the dictate to keep your eyes open when doing *zazen*. When working, neither the eyes nor the mind should wander. The wandering mind was an expression of the ego and therefore had to be uprooted in order to reveal the "True Nature" of who you really were.

In 1974 our touring peaked in a three-month concert tour in Central and South America. By that time I was deeply involved in my world of Zen and was planning to quit the ensemble and join the staff in the Zen Center. Given my tendency to exaggerate everything

I was involved in, I felt that coming to Rochester only two or three times a year would not get me anywhere. So when I was finally allowed to work and participate at the Center as a staff member for roughly a year, I left Collegium Vocale and moved to Rochester for as long as my visa would allow. To make some money, I found a job, based in Cologne but completely flexible, making detailed drawings of prehistoric stone tools for publication by the Institute of Early History at Cologne University. I was allowed to take the little knives and spearheads with me (maybe it was not quite clear to them that "with" meant on a plane to the U.S.) and thus I could still earn a little while spending time at the Center. I wonder what airport security today would make of tiny but sharp stone blades taken on board as important hand luggage.

The Rochester Zen Center was set up in a way that was very much integrated into American culture. American holidays were turned into Buddhist celebrations, if possible, and new ceremonies were developed that embraced both American and Buddhist traditions. I remember a very elaborate New Year's celebration in which we formed a long line, each of us holding a candle that was lighted from the one the *roshi* held out, representing the rekindling of our spiritual relationship with Buddhahood. Formalities and rituals always had significance in relation to Zen practice. The bowing when entering the *zendo* and when meeting the *roshi* was called "bending the mast of ego." The ego was obstructing happiness, fulfillment, and certainly enlightenment: it needed to be banished.

The sculpted figure of a sitting Buddha was the centerpiece of the main *zendo* and, over time, beautiful scrolls or figurines were added and placed in strategic places in the building. Looking at their quiet faces gave me great confidence and comfort in difficult times especially in *sesshin*, the silent retreat week at the heart of Zen training.

Most of the daily work at the Center was physical labor. Normally I found myself immediately evaluating the degree to which my allotted task was to my liking. But obediently I tried to do as I was told and pulled myself back to the actual doing as soon as I noticed distraction from the work at hand. I learned, not immediately but over the next several years, to stay focused on what I was doing and thus lay the groundwork for staying altogether attentive while moving and acting in daily life. But I also developed a definite image of what it meant to do things in the "right" way, and at best I felt sorry for people who did not do *zazen*.

Overhearing a casual remark by one of the senior staff about me, saying "…this is a good one," worked to further my steadfast intention to be a "true Zen person": someone attentive, careful but efficient, kind, freely admitting mistakes, and striving for everybody's happiness…or so I believed. The ability to just enjoy the outcome of something done well or to investigate without judgment why I did something wrong was something I was far from understanding and further from practicing.

Born in a small city in Germany, near the end of World War II, I was raised with typical conditioning to respect order and thoroughness, and I therefore had no problem developing a disciplined attitude towards work at the Zen Center and following it with zeal. I tried to work "wholeheartedly," a term often used, whether I was stuffing cushions with cotton or cutting onions (crying allowed), and I loved polishing the gleaming wooden planks in the hallways and in the *zendo*. The way I was responding to these rules reminds me today of the way the East Germans officially responded to Communism after World War II.

Most meditation practices, and especially the older meditation schools, can be considered as being each one a closed system, which develops its own worldview, raising questions and providing its own answers about what is desirable and how to achieve it. It seems clear that, given a specific model of the world and our role in it, the related exercises, visions, and goals make sense, and at the time I did not even question the claim that with enlightenment I would get the ultimate understanding of "reality." I fully adopted the worldview offered to me and applied it with extreme efficiency to my life. That even went so far as my burning all the concert bills and program notes of my career as a musician and singer. "I won't need this anymore. Aren't I safely on my way to Buddhahood?" My mother helplessly tried to persuade me otherwise but she didn't succeed. She felt very sad about this, as did I many years later.

In the years that followed, I worked mostly in the kitchen, which provided me with great smells, some tasting, and the knowledge of what we would get for dinner. It also gave me a kind of modest pride, if such an oxymoron is possible, since I was aware that working in the kitchen was a serious job and normally given to "developed" practitioners—though I could not quite work out what was so superior in the behavior of the kitchen crew. They were certainly a lively bunch and I was in constant awe of our head cook's cleverness in calculation. As a mathematical illiterate, I was astounded at his ability to work out the proportions for our constantly changing meal numbers, sometimes up to fifty, but more often only twenty-five. I helped prepare lots of dishes I had never tasted before and started to speak English a bit more fluently, in spite of the no-chat rule. I was taught meaningful English phrases like "put an egg in your shoe and heat it," and by using them at times freely, if inappropriately, I contributed to the general amusement. Of course, my English would have improved somewhat faster if I had been reading, but this was not encouraged. Had not the Buddha himself responded to the question "what is truth" by holding up a flower? My understanding was that reading psychology, literature, or philosophy—especially philosophy—was only distracting me from what I needed to do to become a fully developed enlightened being.[4]

I also remember having had a very unfortunate collision with the blade of a Cuisinart. Pulling back my hand with a short scream and finding a fingertip hanging loose, I thought in a haze of pain, "Which garbage bin should this go into, as it's meat" (an important dilemma in a vegetarian kitchen). The "meat" was finally sewn back on by two rather light-hearted doctors who commented cheerfully on how well they were doing their stitches.

At the Center we sometimes had other guests and one regular was a fellow German, named Knut, who made it his specialty to be the fastest dishwasher on the planet. This included his willingness afterwards to mop up the floor, inevitably flooded while he was transferring dishes from one basin to the other. It was customary that once a week more advanced students delivered what was called a "dharma talk," showing their understanding of Zen. I was always mortified by the thought that I would one day have to sit there and wittily demonstrate the depth of my Zen. Yet I remember getting into quarrels with Knut in a kind of mock "dharma-talk," for example over some tomatoes that he had cut open. "Look, look!" he said, "They are all one, like us. Each tomato is just a tomato." And I was yelling back, "But can't you see! They're all different. Each one has completely different patterns and probably not even the same number of seeds in them." Knut: "But nevertheless, they are all tomatoes. The difference is only on the surface." And on we went. Knut was a tall, lean, intense person, frighteningly honest and an idiosyncratic observer. He once pointed out to me, "You know these people here don't even know what bad behavior or true vice is. They are all benign children." Yet, in fact, the difficulties in the social life of many members of the *sangha*, as the Buddhist community is called, led the *roshi* to ask Toni to be a counselor for the problems people had in their relationships with partners, parents, and such.

In my letters to my mother from this time, food played an astonishingly prominent role. In fact food was quite a potent outlet for sensual craving when so much was being demanded of us in terms of self-discipline and other austerities. There was chanting before and after food was served, and the offering of some morsels of food for the hungry ghosts (which, I was told, stood in place of us, being unenlightened and greedy). The effect was that everybody, or at least most of us lowly trainees, tried to eat as much as we could in the given window between the beginning and the concluding chants. This led to a certain kind of frenzy during the common meals, which was not at all ideal Zen behavior. So the decision was made to skip the final chants in order to provide enough time for everybody to eat in peace. Well, peace—being something we mostly bring from within—did not quite manifest itself, since we now felt uneasy about being the last ones sitting at the table and obviously gorging ourselves. But the rule was never repealed and eventually I learned, no, not to eat less, although that would have done me good at the time, but to allow myself to do what I did without the consent of everybody around me.

Nevertheless, eating and diet played important additional roles. One driving factor was that the *roshi* himself had had a stomach ulcer and was very interested in a healthy diet. His comments about the unhealthy diet of white rice that he had been forced to eat in Japan, where the monks successfully resisted the introduction of whole grain rice, led the Center to introduce macrobiotic cooking when I was first in the kitchen, but on my next visit I found that everything had changed and we were making our own yoghurt. It took me a few years to notice that we changed our outlook on healthy eating about every twelve months. It eventually dawned on me that the fervent belief in the diet of the moment as the world's only road to health was perhaps the same trait which I discerned in myself: the need to turn everything into something permanent, true, and unshakeable. I was learning that it was exactly this ideal that does not exist. Applying this insight, banal as it might seem, to every aspect of my life was a slow and painful process and is still going on.

Most of the staff lived in a house nearby, which the Center owned, and for a while I was sharing a room with Polly who did her yoga exercises even before morning *zazen*. So I got up and joined her. We would then walk to the Center for the first sitting at 6 a.m. This was considered a "late" starting time and a concession to the "westernized" style of our Zen affairs, as it was allegedly normal to start at 5 a.m. at least or whatever was considered dawn. (Somehow, I never thought much about what that should really mean in winter.) Our evening *zazen* was usually over by 9:30 p.m. and you could be in bed by 10 p.m. if you wanted to. Sitting brought a gentle quietness back into our lives after a busy day. Although I didn't care so much for the burning incense, the comfort of being in stillness together with my fellow trainees and hearing the bells, the gentle breathing, or rain hitting the windows amidst the silence, was reviving. Afterwards we would often still sit around for a while and chat over a cup of tea. I never got enough sleep and was often so tired in the morning that my sitting consisted mostly of hanging on and waiting for the bell. No wonder breakfast was attacked as a God-send, because it was the first opportunity to replenish our energy.

Meanwhile, with all the attention given to food, there was obviously a need to instill the opposite pole, fasting. In order to "serve the *sangha*" and the community of Rochester—in Mahayana Buddhism, compassion is the biggest educational focus—once a week we trainees would walk along the streets of the city and pick up garbage all day long on an empty stomach. I liked those days because they were usually followed the next evening by a "private" sprint to an ice cream parlor. Only once did I do a real one-week fast—with the usual belief that it would produce not only a "clarified belly" but a clarified mind—but I was still so hung up on food that, even after feeling the comfort and lightness of having nothing in the stomach after many days of not eating, I reverted immediately to taking refuge in, not so much the Buddha, but pizza, pecan pie, and other highly disparaged foods. I have never done any fasting or gone on special diets since then, having truly understood that it is more appropriate for me to eat moderately, and I found out that I enjoyed healthy food much more when I also ate, occasionally, something "off menu" and "forbidden."

Buddhists perceive themselves as "being one" with the universe. This generally entails great concern about the environment and compassion towards every being, sentient or not. When I watched animals in nature or in films, I accepted that killing was part of the natural order, but I could only acknowledge this if dying was seen as natural as well. Yet how realistically could I imagine what it would be to die myself? One episode still lingers vividly in my mind. I was sitting on a bench in a park, delicious scents streaming from the bushes and flowers around me. I felt serenely happy until I woke up to the fact that I was sitting in the middle of a relentless and fierce slaughter of bees. They were being attacked and killed in their hundreds by big, yellow wasps. The ground was already littered with dead bees and I became incredibly upset. I realized it was this special energy of destruction, a kind of blindness, that upset me and left me shaken, but not death as such nor the absence of a moral dimension to it.

Zen has a specific component in its attitude towards death and suffering which is emphasized by a koan in which a Zen monk encounters a woman sitting at the side of the road, holding her dead child in her lap and crying. The monk gives her a slap and says, "Here is something to mourn about." I eventually understood how this koan referred to the enlightened understanding of death and compassion. Like Tibetan compassion meditation (though taught in a different way), an embodied realization of enlightenment will help you to cope with possible discomfort when confronted with cruelty. Yet I never really came to grips with Zen's emphasis on the difference between the absolute—enlightened—and the relative—normal, everyday—understanding of compassion and death.

Nevertheless, far from conquering death and suffering, or even my less ambitious goal of confronting fear in general, my efforts were brought into question when they came to be tested. Being on staff, I had the opportunity to participate in *sesshins* every month. Once, when I had to skip a month because all seats in the hall were filled, I was so upset I went to a meditation retreat house at Colgate University and sat there by myself for the week. Although I certainly experienced the peace and exuberance that often appears when letting go of my worries and usual self-involved ruminations, I was disappointed by my inability to hold on to this quiet contentment under more challenging circumstances. I tried to sit at night in the nearby woods, but being city-born and raised, I became so frightened by the darkness and the strange noises surrounding me that I had to give up and return to my room.

Having observed myself and other people who have gone through Zen training, I would say that we have a tendency for rigorous discipline or managing our lives through will-power. Also, as Zen practice was quite male-dominated in the seventies, the special difficulties of a training that clearly places its emphasis on mental achievement and considers the body as more or less an instrument to this end, was especially daunting for women. I was not the only one whose menstrual cycle was interrupted and, in my case, only returned to normal after I had left the staff.

After my time as staff member at the Rochester Center ended and I moved back to Cologne, I was asked by my friend Dorle, "Why do you have to make your spiritual life so difficult? It really doesn't have to be that way. Why don't you come and meet our teacher. You will get all you need and more just being in his presence." I could only silently scoff at that idea and politely declined her invitation. Although devotion would never be my way of learning about myself, I now wonder, looking back, if sometimes choosing a training method that is the opposite of your natural inclination might not be an interesting way to discover certain peculiarities and idiosyncrasies that normally stay hidden and are reinforced by the training you have unconsciously chosen, like my tendency to do everything with enormous effort. But then I thought how could anything not earned by sweat and suffering be worthwhile. Not only did I feel our approach to spiritual training to be superior to others, but I was also utterly convinced that my specific Zen training was the only correct one and therefore looked down on anyone else's. The simple basic insight that strong investment, be it physical or psychological, almost always creates the need to defend and uphold what you believe in, was not available to me then. Unfortunately, I have come across the very same attitudes in all kinds of spiritual disciplines.

I think I should mention that the circumstances and methods of my training were specific to the direction and type of my Zen school and teacher. Many years later when my husband, Bob, and I compared our respective lives in the context of Zen training— mine under Kapleau and his for a while under Kobun Shino *roshi*'s guidance at the Santa Cruz Zen Center—we had to laugh because, in spite of the general similarities, it was a bit as if we had lived on different planets. But then, even years into my training, I didn't know much about other Zen training centers in America or in Germany, or that what I had taken to be the only way of Zen training was in fact called "boot camp Zen" by other communities in the U.S. Given how heavily we are influenced and formed through our childhood environment, it is certainly understandable that a strong counter-conditioning is necessary to undo basic beliefs, some of which are not even consciously held. To instill doubts about the nature of the "center-I," the "Me," through which we so trustingly perceive and manage the world, is especially challenging. Yet this seemingly inevitable aspect in many spiritual training methods of massive and complete indoctrination began to bother me later, and I asked myself whether it was really necessary to apply these austere routines to such an extent and within such a controlled environment. Of course, at that stage of my training, I was far from doubting anything other than my inquisitive mind.

Chapter 4

More Training

W HENEVER I VISITED THE CENTER, I USUALLY ARRIVED first in Buffalo, staying at Toni's house for a few days and then driving with her to Rochester. Soon, after having gotten a taste of what it was like to participate in the intensive *sesshin* weeks, my stomach would lurch and my hands go cold and clammy as soon as I glimpsed the outline of the city. Fear made my mouth dry and my breathing shallow. Yet inevitably at the beginning of each *sesshin* I was convinced *Yes! This would be the great breakthrough.* And I rushed in with great energy and conviction, only to fail once more and emerge again as an unenlightened being.

By the "damned third day" of a *sesshin*, my vision of "victory" was regularly replaced by the bleakest thoughts of failure, and my joints ached from seemingly endless rounds of sitting with bent knees. By the sixth day, though, as was the case with most people, my mind would be calm and stable and a strong feeling of energy seemed to have gathered in my lower stomach, a location which, in Zen, as well as Asian martial arts, is called the *hara*, the "energy center" of the body. It is believed that without developing this center the mind would not be tamed. By the end of the week, after the closing ceremony, my nervous system, already very highly strung, was close to overload. When the *sesshin* ended, the sudden release from the structured and guided situation meant that my pent-up energy spilled over and I could not help jumping around wildly and, along with most everybody else, talking incessantly after a whole week's enforced silence.

All Zen training, with its emphasis on posture, rules, and hierarchical traditions is structured to support its claim that without *satori* (the Japanese-Buddhist term for enlightenment) or at least a glimpse of it, known as *kensho*, no real understanding of oneself and the universe is possible. Therefore, in those early years, I never associated meditation with anything related to the release of muscle tension or mental relaxation, aspects that play such an important role in today's scientific research into meditation. After all, I had learned to maintain my "practice" during all kinds of upheaval, including periods of physical pain, tension, and discomfort. Of course, within the tradition, sitting in *shikantaza*—quiet attention—would provide ample opportunity for relaxing the body and releasing the mind from churning thoughts and inner arguing. But when I finally, after many years, learned how to do it correctly, it did not change the basic setting of my nervous system. Neither did it lower the high blood pressure which I had developed in my mid-forties. I eventually realized that I needed to explore decisively different approaches to relax my body.

Zen training, as I knew it, used koans and the commentaries of early Zen masters that accompanied them. These are traditional short dialogues between monks and their Zen master which are not easily interpretable. The student's understanding then had to be demonstrated in front of the teacher in the spirit of enlightenment. One had to have at least a moderate experience of *kensho* to be able to show one's grasp of the true meaning of the koan. Therefore a koan was also a tool to "break through" and "attain" *kensho*. The whole exercise is couched in the language of war and battle, only one of the indications of toughness that pervades the whole atmosphere of Zen training. Especially during *sesshin*, the teacher also provides a bit of motivational theater with a combination of sternness and allure. The specific koan that is most often used as an initial or breakthrough practice is the story of a monk asking the teacher about absolute truth, wondering if a dog also has Buddha nature. He is left rebuffed and quite bewildered by the teacher who just shouts "MU." I had been given this koan, with the explanation not to ponder "MU," but to get right to the essence of it. I was to appear before the roshi and show him in a specific way (I had no idea how) my understanding of what "MU" meant and how it expressed my "True Buddha Nature."

Even within the Zen tradition, the relationship between teacher and student may vary with the tasks assigned and the personality of the teacher. In my case, while working on my first koan, it was somewhat tense. Since I actually liked my teacher and wanted to please him I was loath to appear before him (in what was called *dokusan*), bowing again and again with nothing to say—or whatever I was supposed to do to indicate understanding. It got kind of embarrassing. On the other hand there was an atmosphere of urgency in visiting the teacher at least once a day. Going to *dokusan* involved not only me but about thirty other people also working on their first koan, which sometimes led to interesting, not to say amusing, pile-ups. The *dokusan* room was situated upstairs, connected to the main zendo by beautifully waxed wooden stairs. This meant that those who wanted to attend dokusan had to untangle their legs from the sitting position, get up, go upstairs, and grab a seat on the cushions that formed a waiting line. At the first ring of *roshi*'s bell that announced the beginning of the meeting, everybody tried to fly upstairs. This routine inevitably created a bottleneck situation at the bottom of the stairs. Finally, one day we achieved the biggest body sculpture in meditative life. Everybody collided at the foot of the stairs, a haphazard collection of legs and arms and heads sticking out accompanied by muffled grunting, since even then the rule of silence was observed. At least this is how it must have looked to anyone outside—I was in the middle of the logjam. After this remarkable event, the *roshi* limited the number of people allowed to go up at one time.

Once we had safely arrived at the waiting area, we would slowly advance from cushion to cushion towards the door to the *dokusan* room. When you reached the front of the line, you listened for the short, bright ring of the *roshi* ending the previous meeting and responded with an answering ring of the beautiful bell-bowl. I grappled with this feature of *dokusan* for a very long time. I remember, while waiting in line, developing in my mind multiple scenes of how beautifully measured and at one with the universe— or sometimes, how utterly worthlessly and miserably—I would strike the instrument. These very moments before "going in" and the frantic struggle to "stay with my practice" seem now so very far away, but I wonder if they didn't perhaps provide me with the stamina to sustain for longer periods the state of awareness without intention that I learned to appreciate so much later. I really don't know. Probably we always end up extracting from our training the elements that we were generally inclined towards anyhow. What it did not do at the time was to instill in me any sense of what exactly I was grappling with, beyond the general badness of the "ego."

The *kyosaku*, a traditional wooden, flat, arm-length stick, was used to strike the trainees' shoulders with a degree of force appropriate to their build. A student would raise both hands, palm on palm, to request a blow in order to refocus attention. During *sesshin* the stick was used at the discretion of the people assisting the *roshi*, called monitors. Since we were facing the wall, this meant that our attention was roused frequently just by noticing some movement or shadow on the periphery of vision. This kept everyone on their toes, but was also distracting, at least as long as the mind fantasized all kind of notions about what such interactions might mean. Before being hit with the stick, sitters would be tapped on the shoulder so as not to shock or surprise them unduly. The hitting itself was a brief and targeted whack which I experienced in the first years as usually helpful, since it awakened me from wandering thoughts or drowsy mind states. In later years, the sitting places were built up into an elevated dais, making it easier for the monitors to aim the *kyosaku* properly—it works best by striking a specific place on top of the shoulder near the neck, which meant that, from an awkward angle, hitting an ear in passing was a real possibility.

There are many accounts of the importance of a perfect posture during zazen and much emphasis on overcoming physical pain and suffering. And I had read plenty (this being the kind of reading which was seen as helpful). But although attending to the MU koan provided me with a focus during the long hours of sitting, I was left with the question of where or how to find motivation for doing so. One interesting effect of long sitting in meditation is that you are confronted with how your ideas correspond to reality. In my case, and this is true for most, it meant I did not really understand any more why I was doing all this, since pain and fear were so much more real than lofty goals such as "Buddhahood." During the first few years, I would inevitably find myself sobbing for hours on my cushion. Being left in this state, with all its unpleasantness, finally had a sobering effect and I started to investigate more closely what I was doing. Focusing on MU certainly helped to cut off thoughts of self-pity, of wishful thinking (especially desire for the end of the sitting period), or dreaming about the great time I would have *after sesshin*. As such, it was not so different from counting my breath. The additional impetus to make it effective needed to be more personal. A true yearning always lends energy to a task. But what was I yearning for? Mostly to end the pain in my knees and run! Far away. But I stayed.

To keep the energy high in the zendo, people were encouraged to voice their koan out loud at times; MU of course lends itself nicely to being bellowed or hummed, louder and louder. I tried it all. Whispering, humming, yelling it hysterically, whatever I felt the situation was demanding. I felt I should be "deeply involved" and truly "into" my koan. Then I slowly realized that I would not get anywhere if I repeated MU automatically or simply for the sake of being judged a good sitter. I had to find ways for MU to stand for something urgent, something that really was at the core of my motivation. Why was I doing this? I found that behind all my glorious ideas of a life "happy ever after" lay enormous fear. Not the fear of failure, but of being left alone, of having nowhere to turn to, of being literally homeless, which had been a recurrent theme in my life. Only much later did I understand that this also was a real and true scar from a painful childhood experience. I was unconsciously connecting the concept of MU to the possibility of healing the great sadness that I had suffered when, aged four, I was separated from my mother and put into a children's home in Switzerland for a year. So eventually MU was no longer for me the removed idea of "Buddha Nature" or "Oneness" but represented my true home or rather, as I finally realized, eternal security, no less. This realization changed my practice, but of course did not provide an instant solution. It is hard to say if getting some realization of what MU actually meant for me took so long because of my personal obstinacy or the specific circumstances of the training or both. In any case, it took me a full seven years of diligent work to experience *kensho* "officially" and with awareness.

Meanwhile, still under the spell of Zen philosophy, and yearning to attain full Buddhahood or at least a glorious *kensho*, I would sit outside in the garden and let the mosquitoes have me—testing, and thus strengthening, my concentration, so I thought—my blood being my compassionate contribution to the "hungry ghosts" of greed. The insects would bite right through the substantial thickness of my robe, and my knees, after a few days, were so swollen that I could not bend them any more. Nobody at the time pointed out to me that this was more about affirming my self-image of being a good Zen person than dissipating the constant notion of myself as the centerpiece of the world. Every time I stood under the shower, I also would try and get into the "right mind state" for the sudden experience of *kensho*, since I remembered that was what had happened to someone else. The shower itself proved to be an enormous relief from the aches of sitting, but nothing more.

We were all required to wear robes, which were brown, heavy, baggy, and produced equality in appearance. But due to the hierarchical nature of the system, whoever got "through their first koan"—which meant having had an acknowledged *kensho* experience—was allowed to wear a very intricately sewn bib, the *rakusu*, a part of the Japanese tradition that was upheld at the Center. So even with demurely averted eyes I could not help noticing the lucky ones who obviously had an easier life than myself, sitting in serenity and without constant fear of appearing before the teacher or being caught dreaming by the stick-wielding monitors. I was stung by jealousy whenever I was confronted with someone wearing a rakusu and doubled my efforts to be the next to win one, at the same time condemning myself heartily for this reaction. The distraction and emotional tumult this custom aroused (and not only in myself) was never really addressed; I suspect it was even encouraged as a means to enforce the eagerness to practice. Toni and I finally spoke about this when we were no longer teacher and student and started communicating on a more equal level. We both felt that accommodating the ancient hierarchical structure and using a reward system was at best unhelpful and often a real hindrance to clarity of mind.

Yet there were also the serene moments of just sitting and being part of the sounds around me: the breathing, the wind rattling the windows, sometimes the cardinal bird's persistent pleas of woe from a branch nearby. There was stability and peace—at least until this feeling was noticed by that ever-vigilant inner commentator of the busy mind and pounced on like a spider detecting a catch in its net.

Were these extreme efforts really worth the results they produced? There is no simple answer. I found out later that there were many different, and also less radical, ways to experience some degree of undivided awareness. Some people even come to this remarkable but, as I have said before, not unnatural state of awareness without any conscious preparation at all. But it remains a question if the specific circumstances of this form of training were not actually a hindrance to the very goal that it presented to us. In my case, some of the characteristics of the regime may have been damaging to my health. Yet, for someone with a much more stable nervous system and less inclined to an overly demanding self-discipline, this system of training the mind might be beneficial. It certainly helped develop in me a mental stamina that was trapped in difficult personal experience and painful life circumstances.

Tenacious as I was in my quest for the true answer, I was equally persistent in my stupidity. But then, one day, after stumbling around in a kind of haze and literally not knowing where I was much less what I was doing, this changed and I was left at last with some kind of lever to get a different view of what was going on in my mind from moment to moment.

Chapter 5

Thunder

THERE IS ALWAYS EMPHASIS IN THE BUDDHIST TEACHINGS ON the impossibility of putting certain experiences into words and therefore that any attempt will be an inevitable failure. Yet, by using and sharing such words as "Oneness" or "Buddha Nature" and especially "enlightenment," these words and concepts become inextricably intertwined with the experience and turn into a reality that we think we share with one another. It can be compared to meeting for the first time someone who has the same name as a close friend. The name has so melded with the person we already know that it takes a conscious effort to apply it to the new person just met. Only in many circumstances we are not even aware of doing this. The question of how to deal with the impossibility of sharing experience without creating new fixed concepts became more and more interesting and challenging to me as I started to come upon new states of consciousness.

My very first little encounter with a curious new form of perception was while meditating—I can no longer recall if it was in a *sesshin* or just a general daily *zazen* round in the main hall. As usual I was sitting facing a wall. I was suddenly aroused by a creaking of the floor. I became aware that I, while clearly perceiving a sound, had not immediately produced an image of a walking person or the boards under his feet or of *anything* for that matter. This was new and a very puzzling experience, as our instinctive mode of response compels us to draw on our memory and emotional validation with every perception we encounter, even if we are usually completely unaware how we compose an event from a mix of input and internal interpretation. I was stunned because I realized that I did not automatically need to react to what I perceived. For a moment I was quite absorbed in the implications this incident provided for me. But somehow I was so surprised that I did not relate it to the context of my training at the time or the philosophical framework I was using then.

Some time later, another incident, somewhat different in character, occurred while I was walking around in Buffalo with some friends and talking about my mother who was at the time living in Germany. All of a sudden I had an insight of "my mother" being at this moment nothing but a thought, an inner picture, an image, fabricated entirely by my personal accumulated specific knowledge of her. It completely stunned me. This insight later had a strong effect on how I reacted to her dying and the way I remembered her.

When I came to a more solid and prolonged experience of non-dual awareness, the typical preconditions were in place: sleep deprivation and long periods of focused energy had allowed for a moment of intense stillness and I "woke up" literally to lightning and thunder. I was sitting in the hall. It was early evening and a huge thunderstorm was moving through the area. There was light and dark and sound and vibration and a blank wall, all in one. The sounds were not different from the light, it came from no direction, no space. No center. No body. The wall was what amused me most. How come I had never looked at it? Such a blank wall! So amazing to look at. After a little while I realized, "That's it!" I had done it! I finally knew what MU was all about. A wave of giddy exhilaration washed over me and I couldn't wait to get up and run into the roshi's room and be tested. When I met with him I was very, very happy.

Outside the rain was streaming down and, among other things that I have forgotten, he was asking me, "Can you stop the rain?"

I looked at him in confusion: "But, but there is nobody there to stop anything...and...and...rain isn't..."

I could not find the words. And finally: "But I am all that rain!"

And after a little while, somewhat helpless: "But there is nothing there anyway!"

When he smiled but didn't say anything, I just lay down on the floor as if enjoying getting showered by the drops, making the noise of the rain with my lips. I also started to cry at some point, which I later recognized as tears of incredible relief and also nerves finally failing to hold up. With time I came to understand that I had, through the preparation and environment I was primed with, reacted in a specific way to experiencing what is called in the Zen tradition *kensho* or, more widely now, non-dual awareness, where the distinction between self and non-self, the duality of experience, dissolves in a form of pure awareness.

At the end of *sesshin*, having built up an immense amount of energy, I was able to stay in this specific mind state for longer periods. When the *sesshin* was over, I went with a group of people who welcomed me into their club of "post-Muers" to a small lake after finishing the last meal. I was still so energized and "high" that I swam across the whole lake and back in one happy moment, not realizing that it had taken probably twenty minutes and the others were waiting and starting to worry. Although being proud of having "advanced" to the "knowers" was seen as not proper, since it related to the ego that was supposedly shattered through the opening of the "mind's eye," somehow the emphasis on achievement in Zen—and perhaps not only Zen but in other disciplines as well or, for that matter, all traditions—seems to foster this attitude.

Nevertheless, very soon I started to wonder how to put this precious ability to work in my life and why, since it was such a big achievement and truly felt good, it somehow got lost when the struggles of daily living took over. The common explanation went: We revert out of habit. To achieve a permanent state of enlightenment you had to change towards being a better human being. Once you were finally an egoless person—perhaps after innumerable lifetimes—you would be seen as fully enlightened.

This was, as I later discovered, a grave mental error but dominated my life for a long time. Zen strongly emphasizes the necessity of integrating our normal life, which is always driven by a specific viewpoint—me—with the experience of a non-dual awareness—an experience of no standpoint at all—and not only in Zen. Many psychological tendencies that we all share and that are seen as an expression of ego were addressed mostly by working through two big koan collections, the *Mumonkan* and the *Hekiganroku*.[5] Some of these koans deal with reactions to praise or disparagement or falling for flattery, experiencing pain or simply allowing for a quick gut reaction without standing in the way with long "heady" evaluations. Within the Zen tradition a sequence of artful paintings, the "ox pictures," illustrates how to achieve this integration of the relative (the daily life with its inward and outward relationships) and the absolute (the experience of non-relation or oneness). Or rather, they indicate what it should look like, implying that there is a progressive development ending "in abiding unassertively in a state of unshakable serenity."[6] The fact that I never met anyone with that quality or gained it myself only meant, from the Zen point of view, that I had not "attained full enlightenment"— nothing further to discuss.

I finally enjoyed sitting through further *sesshins* in *"shikantaza,"* attentive and without monitoring the thoughts and feelings wandering through—what is called mindfulness in other disciplines. Often I would glide, without intention, into non-dual awareness. Also, whenever I became aware of especially strong emotional upheaval and stayed quietly with it, I would (again often involuntarily) switch into a non-dual awareness and, with it, the whole process of involvement came to an abrupt end. The experience of stillness and the brilliance of the environment, when simply sensing it without evaluating it or reacting to it, is very special and precious. It never became dull over the years, though, as it became an ever-larger part of my life, I no longer felt the excitement or specialness of the first encounters.

Comfortable in my newly found peace and the beauty of sitting in inner and outer silence, I was not very eager to deal with the many koans that followed and that were part of generations of Zen training. You had to interpret these short dialogs or utterings in a specific traditional Zen manner. "A cow goes through a window, why doesn't the tail goes through?" may have many meanings aside from the basic understanding coming from the actual experience of "oneness." The constant flickering of the tail keeping away the flies, for example, can be seen as depicting constant thinking and the urge to solve problems (the flies also seen as thoughts) by more thoughts. Some of the koans that preceded the ones in the *Mumonkan* will stick forever in my mind, more because of my somewhat limited command of the English language than new insights into daily life. One had a phrase in it about "raining cats and dogs," and I labored forever with the image of cats and dogs coming down from the sky and whether this had a specific meaning until the roshi enlightened me that it was simply an idiom for heavy rain and was not necessarily pointing me to intricacies like meowing or barking while being a human being. Another had to do with acting appropriately in a situation, in this case imprisonment in a dungeon—yelling for help, rather than sitting in quiet bliss. Unfortunately I imagined a dungeon as a luxurious kind of castle and consequently felt no need to escape or call for help. Yet some of those preliminary koans—like the one that asked about "entering a spoon"—were easy to demonstrate, for in Zen the student's understanding is often not articulated verbally and it would not suffice to give an intellectual explanation, such as "a non-dual state has no conceptual limitation."

But these were really only marginal phenomena and the real and true challenge consisted of finding again and again this precious state of mind in which everything seemed to take care of itself. Due to the specific situation of focused energy during *sesshin*, it was much easier in those weeks than during the regular routine of daily tasks. Entering this state, which we also called "an open mind," had been especially easy after my initial breakthrough. As I discovered, over time it would vary greatly as to when and how I could get back into it. However, I did not feel so much the openness as much as its opposite—the daily clutter of associations, judgments, and unconscious moods washing through me, making me feel like what Toni sometimes called the "broom closet of ego."

One of the subtle but successful ways of switching into openness, whether during sitting or in daily life, was using certain words or phrases that had brought it on before. For instance, I remember that for a while I would call out voicelessly "home" and instantly the mind opened up, usually not for very long, but repeatedly. Somehow the effectiveness of these particular words dried up over time and I had to find new ones that my mind would somehow associate with that state and bring it about.

When Knut and I had rather mockingly referred to our tomatoes as being one and different, neither of us had experienced what it meant; with *kensho*, the concept of "Oneness" indeed proved rather disturbing to me. Repeatedly I would be in this non-dual state and not find anything to be one with or a "me" to do so. The phrase "to be one with the universe" just did not hold up very well. Wasn't "the universe" a fabrication of the mind? And for that matter, when listening to or seeing a bumblebee, I might be in a state of "oneness," not experiencing the division of subject-object, but neither did I have any feeling or experience of flying around and make sounds with "my" wings.

Meanwhile I was more or less successfully plowing through the *Mumonkan*, encountering its medieval Chinese fist-swinging and mind-pummeling characters. The questions that were addressed were often profound, such as how I understood the concept of cause and effect. But since the koans, the dialogues, and situations they depict initially had developed in a monastic setting and dealt mostly with men, they translated rather clumsily into everyday life and were not really very direct. Even later, when still laboring further through the *Mumonkan* with Toni, this tradition did not seem to connect to my daily life as much as I wanted it to do.

Chapter 6

Learning to Learn

A S I AM WRITING, I CAN PICTURE TONI MANY YEARS LATER, lying in her hospital bed in her home in the Finger Lakes region, south of Rochester, her eyes tracing the noisy gathering of birds at the feeder, which she can see through a big window looking out onto a meadow. Bed-ridden and in constant pain, she appeared sharp and composed when I last visited her. She was still the head of her own meditation center—now known as Springwater Center—founded 30 years earlier.[7] Toni and, later, the philosopher and spiritual teacher Jiddhu Krishnamurti were my most sustaining influences, until the time when I needed to question the framework of teaching non-dual awareness altogether.

Toni had started to train with Kapleau *roshi* soon after he opened his center, not long before we met in 1971. After she completed the necessary training requirements, she was the first person that *roshi* asked to become a teacher. Over the course of many years, during my frequent stays with her family, our traveling together and exchanging insights, Toni became my mentor and close friend.

In the earlier days, we sometimes went to a small piece of land Toni and her husband Kyle owned and we strolled along a little creek that was part of this landscape. One day, when Toni and I were walking quietly, an airplane flew noisily overhead and she asked me innocently how far away in the sky I thought it was. I remember being puzzled by her question and said, "Why do you ask?"

"Well do you think it's a big plane or a small one? How do you judge that?"

We walked on a bit, the sound of the plane slowly receding. I stood and looked around. "But…but the plane, how do I know? It seems the sound could have come from anything or anywhere."

Toni said, "Yes, yes! So?"

I looked at her helplessly. "So what?"

She sighed.

On another occasion, a few years later, we had lunch outside and my lower arm was resting on the surface of a wooden table. The air was very still and the sounds of nature were all around us.

I looked at my arm and remarked, "You know, my arm and the table are not really different."

To anybody in their right mind this would sound like a pretty silly utterance. But Toni's ears pricked up, she looked at me sharply and said, "Yes, of course! Do you understand?"

I looked at her and after a little silence said, "Hmm…no." I watched her expectantly.

She looked at me with mild irritation and said, "You know, you are quite thick-headed. Your imagination really is preventing you from your own obvious insights."

I now understand what Toni meant: I was so eagerly pursuing enlightenment as something other than what presented itself at that moment and therefore did not notice when I was actually experiencing it.

One day, I came down the stairs into their living-room humming, and she, sitting on the sofa, looked up and said, "So, just now, was there somebody who hummed and found herself attractive doing that or was there someone showing how happy she was?" I was stunned. What? I just stood there thinking. I now recall that, in this case, there was no such image in my mind, but this conversation stayed with me. How subtly, or for that matter not so subtly, is my self-image guiding my behavior? This was a question I learned to pose silently and which I later came to appreciate as very valuable. I learned to detect when I acted and argued from an "ego"-driven point of view, expending lots of energy defending myself, making myself loveable, appearing knowledgeable, and so on. Only much later did I begin to think how interesting it would be to investigate what this "ego" actually is and why we develop such a tendency for playing games with ourselves and with each other in the first place.

After I had finally understood what *kensho* meant and was working on other koans, I complained to Toni about the *roshi's* rejection of some of my answers. She said, "I know what you mean. It is not necessarily wrong what you did or said in response to this koan but you have to be aware that Zen has developed a specific language, or rather communicative framework, that one has to use properly to pass the koan, even if you grasp the essence of it quite thoroughly." I was dumbfounded. I was still thinking in terms of "absolute truth" and had not reflected on the fact that even if we all agreed that it existed, it would have to be communicated in a specific form.

Toni and I also started exchanging observations that had little specific Zen flavor. Once she said, "This is curious. When I light a candle at the altar I notice that I make kind of a little grimace, pressing my mouth together or something. But I realize that whenever I do this I am actually not in open awareness but in some little cubbyhole of ego, commenting on what I do or even on something else." This was most interesting and I could easily confirm this in myself, observing it in my own life in many different situations, whether I was cutting bread, hammering a nail into a wall, scrubbing a dish, or whatever. On the other hand, doing these actions with a quiet "open" mind would leave my face relaxed and quiet.

Yet I also had to learn to discern remarks that were just personal and not connected to non-dual awareness in any way. We were walking together along a green hillside, when Toni made a very negative statement about the plastic sheeting covering some bales of hay, saying that it stuck out, white and alien in the otherwise bucolic landscape.

I said, "But why would it disturb you when you are in an 'open mind' state?"

And she answered, "But it disturbs the landscape."

Another remark also left me confused, as I was only then starting to realize that I tended to project infallibility into her answers. Toni had a good singing voice and had sung semi-professionally in her youth. But, when I knew her, she had stopped, and one day I asked her, with some concern for my own career, "What happens to creativity when I am through?"—our slang for "through my first koan"—"Will I still be interested in art? In singing? Will I be capable of being creative?"

Her answer was, "You will see for yourself." But a little later she added, "You won't need it."

Yet she was also encouraging me to question established attitudes about correct behavior or procedures at the Zen Center that I had taken for granted. One was the training and, eventually, the capacity to stay in a non-dual mind state when dealing with pain or discomfort, and therefore remaining undisturbed by it. Sometimes during *sesshin*, the sound of the stick hitting the shoulders could be heard quite often, and one day Toni remarked that no matter how open and non-dual her mind state was, these constant sharp sounds had an effect on her body and were making her jumpy. I often thought about this remark later, when I was living in New York once again and the roar of the city and its grinding noise tired me no end. It helped me understand the difference between a situation that, if bothersome, can be changed and perhaps should be, and one that I have no control over (at least at the moment) and to which I could therefore apply non-dual awareness to remain undisturbed.

After she started doing counseling, Toni told me that she felt more and more that practicing *zazen* really seemed to have little effect on people's understanding and their ability to solve their everyday life problems. Later, when she was already a Zen teacher, she explained to me the doubts she had about her whole involvement in the Buddhist tradition. She realized, for example, that many of the people talking to her in private meetings were actually believing in and relying on the Buddha to help them to become enlightened. She was thoroughly put off by this, since it went deeply against her understanding of shedding the fetters of mental dependencies and becoming psychologically self-reliant. Eventually, through her questioning and probing, I allowed myself to doubt also and to scrutinize the many features of the Zen training I had undergone for so many years.

Toni's doubts about the relevance of Zen teaching coincided with, or perhaps were partly caused by, her discovery of the writings of the Indian philosopher and spiritual teacher Jiddhu Krishnamurti, who rejected all authority with regard to spiritual seeking. Toni and her husband Kyle had become avid readers of Krishnamurti's books and traveled to many places to hear his public talks. Sometimes I joined them. Once we met in England to attend one of his big gatherings. I remember seeing him as a thin, little man sitting modestly on a simple chair in front of probably five hundred people and, as I worded it to myself, "radiating pure love." Of course I am not the only one who has ever projected my ideals and imaginings onto a suitable figure. I was enthusiastic and energized and did not notice that Toni's admiration went even further than mine.

I eventually learned to observe how I was projecting infallibility onto teachers or systems, and was therefore inevitably disappointed time after time. Toni, after becoming aware of the projection problem regarding teachers, stayed adamant that she was not a teacher when she was head of the Springwater Center. But this was a rather empty claim, as she was the heart and brains of her Center and hesitated a long time before allowing some of her well-trained students to take over teaching. Through this and similar experiences, the question of what it means to be a teacher in any of the so-called spiritual disciplines became a prevailing interest of mine with the consequences I describe in later chapters, though my decisions differed from Toni's. With time, I understood that I could and would never again idolize a teacher or any person. And, eventually, I myself would stop teaching.

The main thrust of Krishnamurti's teachings concerns the negative aspects and consequences of religious belief systems and attachment to national identities. However, what I learned through him most importantly was of another nature. I was more and more able to stop and listen without preconception or, as he liked to say, "without choice," to ongoing internal activities. In other words, by learning to observe without judgment, or rather also observing the judgment of my own behavior, I would discover, and in time change to some degree, some of my normally unconscious, fixed, and unproductive ways of dealing with life situations. This was what Toni and I considered "learning," as opposed to "training," which we thought of as practicing with preset goals that are not questioned. In Zen, for example, I had specifically trained to act with kindness and compassion according to a particular moral code. Now, instead, I tried to learn what often prevented me from being a kind person and neither condemning nor praising myself, whatever the outcome.

Krishnamurti constantly reminded you of the necessity for inner stillness, "the Other," as he called non-dual awareness. He was convinced you need the presence of this special awareness in order to observe your conditioning. Waiting in line for admission to his talks, I often overheard conversations that made it clear to me that many people who were listening to him, and even followed him around, never seemed to have experienced what he referred to. These observations supported my conviction that listening to talks was not enough, and that quiet retreats, a staple of both Zen practice and what had become Toni's teaching approach (or as she preferred to call it "doing the work"), were an important aid to accessing non-dual awareness.

Toni's family owned an apartment near Gstaad in Switzerland, which I was invited to use. This gave me the opportunity to listen to several of Krishnamurti's talks as he spoke there frequently. These summer days are among my happiest memories and only surpassed later by hiking in silence with my husband in the beautiful national parks of Utah. The talks were held in a big tent, just as in England, and in the afternoon I often meandered through the mountains. I noticed that I could not refrain from moving on to look around the next bend and see what lay beyond, and the very same thing happened when I came upon a view obstructed by a looming peak. I had to move on and on and often found myself so tired that I barely had the strength to make it back. I knew I could eliminate this impulse by applying a moment of non-duality. But I didn't. In spite of the possibility of moving in the beauty of inner silence and the timelessness of a non-dual mind state, I was overjoyed and excited with experiencing the bracing fresh air, the sound of rushing water, the wild flowers, the smells, the views—all on my personal "ego-bound" level.

Every morning, when the tent finally opened to let us in for the talk, I was in the same quandary. Here I was, quite composed, with a still, open mind, breathing the chilly pine-scented air and ready to enter with dignity and poise. You'd think! But people so badly wanted the front seats that the moment the entrance curtain was moved aside they rushed and slid and elbowed their way in to claim the favored seats. I also wanted to sit close to "K," very much so.

What to do? Should I run with everybody else and behave greedily or let go of my desire and walk, poised and polite, to a back seat? Somehow a non-dual mind state didn't help me arrive at a good solution: while in it, the urge to run was extinguished, but as soon as I was back in my normal state a few moments later, I regretted not being in front and securing a seat near the platform where K was sitting. I usually ended up running, partly being shuffled along with the crowd. Sometimes I managed to walk and sometimes I even got a good seat despite not rushing. All this was trivial, but it led me to consider the role of non-dual awareness in normal life situations.

Once, when standing in line to get in, I caught sight of a very nice-looking young man. Since waiting allowed for leisure and free time, I could observe very carefully a whole succession of events taking place in my mind over the next few days. First, I noticed that his face had struck me as special because I particularly like a face with high cheekbones, and it reminded me of a former lover. Immediately, I was wondering what nationality he might be. At the same time, I was wondering if he would ever look in my direction and perhaps notice me. Whereupon I immediately imagined how I would look into his eyes and then proceeded to rearrange my hair with my hand. Later, at home, I had fantasies about how one morning I would stand directly behind him in my pretty blue t-shirt getting involved in a conversation and, perhaps, how he would even touch my hand in passing. And on it went. Every day, when I was back in the line, I immediately started looking for him. Eventually I became aware of how, to the particular present moment, I was adding the images of him which I had remembered and nursed into extended life-forms during the previous few days. I had built "a little village" of events, scenes, and images, in which I "moved" around and which had very little or nothing to do with what was actually going on. In fact, this attractive man never noticed me, and nothing of what I had spent so much energy fantasizing about and projecting ever happened. I was, however, able to notice two things: one—although I was aware of these mental gymnastics, I was not able to stop them effectively, and two—I became more attentive to the way we produce a world by ourselves, a world that we consider real and independent from ourselves.

This last observation was reinforced strongly by another incident that happened a little later, while I was staying at a friend's house in Basel. When the doorbell rang, I stepped into the hallway and peered down the stairs, curious to see who was coming up. Three men approached. I looked at them and noticed that they were of different heights and one seemed to be older. The man on the right wore a strange, patterned shirt. This observation happened in a fraction of a second. Right then, my friend Maja came out, looked at the men and cried, "Oh, my father! Look, my father is here!" and pointed at the older man. With this the older man changed before my eyes into a fully fledged image of Maja's father, who was a surgeon, who had sent her those wonderful books about the rain forest, who had taken her to her first swimming lesson, whom I had spoken to the other day on the phone, whose voice I found rather pleasant, and whom I had pictured rather differently. This again happened in an instant. But the shift of view almost felt like a landslide. Of course everybody has moments like these. It's the kind of experience you have, for example, when you come back up to the street at a subway station and feel completely disoriented and then, woosh, everything falls into place and the same features that you looked at a moment ago in bewilderment now appear familiar and right. This had happened to me many times, but was what felt familiar and right necessarily real?

More and more, Toni and I came to question the legitimacy given to authority in Zen training as we knew it. How could one think and act independently when, at the same time, one was expected to adopt the perspectives of the patriarchs, which were transmitted through a variety of ways, including two volumes of koan collections, commentaries, talks, and so forth? Because of Toni's change of attitude and the influence of Krishnamurti's teaching, I was the first student who went to the *roshi* and told him that I wanted to continue my koan study with Toni. I was probably about a quarter of way through the *Mumonkan*. I always had a good relationship with the *roshi* and he was not disconcerted by this request but suggested, in a very kind manner, that I should at least finish the *Mumonkan* with him, as Toni was not yet so experienced in teaching koans. I remember how I took a deep breath and, in spite of some kind of love for him welling up, stood my ground and insisted that that was what I needed to do. Very soon after this, Toni and I would engage with each other, even during official meetings, much more as equals, dropping the koan study altogether and instead starting to look directly at whatever was of importance to me at that moment. For example, we talked about the feeling of self-importance that would creep up when I felt that I was being hit unnecessarily with the *kyosaku* stick, or my embarrassment when I noticed this feeling. I learned to see this and the accompanying annoyance as unnecessary and energy-consuming rather than as right or wrong. I could therefore better separate the actual situation from my personal involvement, and I was able to ask politely but firmly not to be hit any more with the stick. More generally, I also learned to observe and differentiate emotions that surfaced not because of a specific situation but because of accumulated stress.

Toni finally summoned the courage to decide that she could no longer support teaching the philosophy and psychology of formal Zen. At this time, in the late seventies, I too was already distancing myself from the formal attitude of the Rochester Zen Center, and I encouraged her to leave. I remember the long meetings she had with the *roshi* and her nervousness and doubts about symbolically defying the long line of patriarchs and Zen masters. I now believe that this is far from being a trivial issue. When breaking with a tradition of this magnitude, a person not only stands alone, with no outside guidance or support, but is confronted with enormous doubts about his or her own capability and judgment—an individual's own understanding or wisdom compared to a seemingly endless line of "spiritual" giants. Fortunately, the *roshi* and Toni did not part ways in a hostile manner, but he certainly did not seem to understand Toni's concerns. And this amicable act of separation was repeated between Toni and myself much later, when I quietly but decisively ended my relationship with her as her assistant and successor in teaching.

Chapter 7

Interlude in Poland

BEING ON SUCH INTIMATE TERMS WITH TONI AND CONSIDER-ing my respect and high regard for Krishnamurti's teaching and perspective, having already organized sitting groups and having assisted Toni with many retreats, it was only natural that I agreed when she asked me to assist in her teaching. I worked mainly in Europe and my experiences as a teacher in Poland played an important role in how my understanding of consciousness, meditation, and even non-dual awareness evolved, right from when I joined Toni conducting retreats there in the late seventies.

I had already met the Polish Buddhist community through a curious incident many years before. This was the time when Poland was still behind the Iron Curtain and Western influence was tightly monitored. Even typewriters had to be registered, and a copy machine in private hands was certainly suspicious. Yet some writers and poets had discovered *The Three Pillars of Zen* and had translated it into Polish. They had secretly made copies and distributed them between their friends. In due course they contacted the Rochester Center and wrote letters asking for clarification of certain points. Their many serious questions meant that the *roshi* felt compelled to acknowledge their eagerness to learn more. Just at that time my vocal ensemble was invited to do a concert in Warsaw, which provided the first opportunity to contact them in person, and I, though still very new in the training myself, was briefed on what I should teach them and how. So it happened that I arranged a clandestine gathering in my hotel, thus staging the first official "Zen meets Poland" event.

Working on the assumption that the only unsuspicious sign we had in common to recognize each other was the stylized three-pillar calligraphic logo on the cover of the book, I went down into the lobby and placed the book carefully on a little table with my sweater covering the English title, leaving only the logo visible. And to my astonishment after only a short time a middle-aged woman and an older man with an unkempt beard appeared. He smiled and rather briskly picked up the book, equally careful not to show the whole book jacket, took my elbow, maneuvered me outside, and we started walking. This was as far as any Cold-War-style espionage tactics went but it had a lasting effect, because it made me aware of the threat of persecution, which was confirmed later by my hosts, and how the suspicion of spies and surveillance was never far away in those days.

The Polish *sangha* was a gregarious bunch of people, mostly artists, writers, and poets. They were exhilarating in their enthusiasm, a mix of fun and seriousness. I was treated with effusive kindness and their hospitality had no limits. As a Westerner, it unfortunately took me a long time to realize how far they would go to fulfill a wish as simple as asking for some honey in my tea. I eventually discovered that, in order to find honey, somebody had to get up very early in the morning and travel to another town nearby and search the market because there had been a rumor that one could find honey there. Similar intricacies had to be mastered when I mentioned that it would be nice to have some lemon in my chamomile tea. I learned eventually to adhere to their diet of cottage cheese, *kasha*, and lots of cabbage in various forms. Potatoes were not so easy to get. I was later astonished to find out that they were mostly shipped to West Germany, apparently for foreign exchange. True to the Buddhist spirit we were all vegetarians including, supposedly, the dog belonging to my hosts—a huge, pitch black, extremely friendly animal that, as I observed one day much to his owners shock and dismay, supplemented its diet by killing and eating rabbits in a nearby field.

Our *kyosaku* demonstration was met with vigorous hands-on enthusiasm and I still have a little black-and-white photograph where I am in the midst of a group of eagerly involved people being hit, while the look on my face is not relaxed, to say the least. I also taught them how to chant, how many times to ring the bell, how to do the clappers, and other formalities of Zen sitting.

Polish people generally seem to have a strong sense of devotion. Whether this has to do with the country's long and intense relationship with Catholicism I don't know, but it certainly showed in the way that even something as austere as Zen was undertaken. They put up and decorated an altar that looked rather like a Tibetan Buddhist shrine, with shelf upon shelf stacked with bowls of foods and flowers and incense, all topped with a Buddha figure. During one of my visits many years later I was again confronted with this pious attitude. My concern about the danger of being caught in the material trappings of religious practice had increased over the intervening years, so I unwittingly behaved rather like one of the old Zen teachers in my eagerness to rid them of what I judged as a completely unnecessary waste of energy. We started to recite the Heart Sutra and, as soon as they were saying the words "no eye, ear, nose, tongue," I grabbed one of the apples on the altar and bit into it with relish and a big munching noise, yelling, with my mouth full, "Am I eating an apple or not? Do you hear me yelling at you or not? Do I taste this apple or not? What are you mumbling about no tongue, no eyes? Aren't you using your tongue right there? Who of you knows what the hell you are talking about? Really?! Truly?!" They looked at me wide-eyed and with concern, since the translation, of course, lagged somewhat behind. When they finally caught on, the chanting faltered. I prodded them further, "Don't stop! Just do it without your tongue. Go on! Do it!" They slowly resumed. I don't know if they understood anything of what I was after and, for myself, I felt I was perhaps in a bit over my head, though I knew and understood perfectly well what it meant to taste or see in emptiness. However, I, like many other teachers I have witnessed, tended to use my authority as a teacher to surprise and shock students. This was not a conscious misuse of power but done in creativity and good-will. But did it help? Or did it instead project their teacher as being so infallible that she could do such things with this kind of chutzpah?

After Toni separated from the Rochester Zen Center, we kept going to Poland, either together or alternately, to conduct retreats. I have two very fond memories from this time. One is of Toni and me incessantly munching on peanuts, probably to compensate for the familiar foods we were deprived of. The other, one of many strange experiences we had in Poland, occurred late one night. We had already turned off the lights when we heard a heavy thumping and breathing, even moaning, and in stumped a young man—hair disheveled, clothes battered, and eyes shining and glittering. Seeing us, he stood and blurted out, "I know, I know now! I have seen it. I have seen enlightenment." Toni and I looked at each other quite helpless. Toni finally said, "All right, but that's no reason to blast in here in the middle of the night. Go and sit a bit longer and then come back tomorrow morning." The young man slowly shrank back and walked out of the room, and he was quite docile and sober next morning when we looked for him. Over time, the people we met in Poland through teaching meditation or, as Toni put it, "meditative inquiry" became good friends, and we were both very fond of them. Ironically, given their eagerness always to hear more, it was with these open and enthusiastic people that I led my last retreat.

Soon after Toni's departure from the traditional forms and rituals of Zen teaching, she started to feel her way into her own kind of teaching, rejecting ceremonies and any appearance of ritual practice. Coming from a discipline so strongly oriented to intense sitting meditation, we did not doubt the benefit of long sitting hours in silence. In her talks and private meetings, Toni also adopted Krishnamurti's approach of posing questions that would motivate students to inquire, for example, whether it was possible to look at a person, a tree, a river without forming a judgment or for that matter a concept at all. Over time, I incorporated many attitudes and images of her teachings into my own repertoire. She asked, for example, if one can look at a flower "not knowing" what it is. She had the gift of bringing into her talks moments of silence and listening without forming associations or judgments. She kept the notion that the "ego" or, as it was called later, the self-image got in the way of pure stillness and had to be "seen." In fact her whole teaching system was based on "seeing" as being the equivalent of "revealed truth." "If a hurt occurs, or a flattery, neither need be milked. Neither need be carried over. The whole thing can drop lightly on its own. There need be no conscious intention to do so. It happens when there's pure seeing that is wisdom."[8] She also was extremely sharp in pointing out moments where a situation involved unconscious emotional coloring, cunning self-defense, or attachment to a certain way of presenting oneself, albeit unawares.

Once, when I was walking with her and some of her Polish students, we came upon a big furry caterpillar slowly traversing the dirt path. Everybody stopped and kneeled or looked down at it and started a lively conversation about how pretty it was and what it was called. Toni coming closer listened and looked and finally said, "Look at it silently. Truly not knowing what it is. Can you not only not know its name but not know anything about it or what it is? Do we really always have to name everything, put our personal seal on it? What is this if I don't know it?" She was pointing out that naming or recognizing something is never completely void of accompanying associations and emotions, and prevents us seeing it in silence and "as it is."

Over time, noticing this habit of naming things and events brought about a moment of non-dual awareness. This attitude was a useful tool, and it was interesting to identify this process of immediately categorizing, naming, and judging what one perceives and then letting go of it completely, thus instigating a truly silent and lively moment of direct sensing. Yet it presented itself to me as a subtle judgment about curiosity. It somehow diminished the value of learning names and meanings, constraining a part of me that appreciated and was stimulated by scientific inquiry. I realized that it kept me from learning more not only about plants but about any other phenomena I was encountering.

Chapter 8

Learning to Question

THE SPECIFIC BENEFITS OF MEDITATIVE INQUIRY AND ITS possible limitations were not the only issues that started to occur to me in those early days in my role as Toni's assistant and then as a teacher. I also began to have doubts about some of the underpinnings of this practice. These came to the surface when, at one of the retreats, I climbed the wooden stairs to where Toni stayed. It had snowed, and the snow was accumulating and stuck to the soles of my boots. This made me rather clumsy, and I made rumbling noises coming up the stairs. Opening the door, I overheard an annoyed Toni making a remark about the insensitivity of walking so loudly. She was always pointing out how one could enhance attention by turning a door knob with utter care or closing a drawer noiselessly and so on, as in her view inattention is a symptom of ego involvement. After looking at "myself" being hurt by the injustice (I had in fact tried to walk quietly), I let it go but a real disquieting thought bothered me: Do we really know anybody's state of mind when they are doing something? Can we really judge simply by observing behavior? This is not a trivial question, and I felt compelled to investigate it later and go beyond the common explanation that we just learn to read or interpret other people's activities by body language, vocal expression, or deeds. How DO we judge, know, "see," what ego or self-image is? Is it possible at all?

Does it depend on how we define it?

Around this time, I went through a very painful separation from my long-time partner, and I needed all the psychological skill which I had acquired from my previous training to cope with the onslaught of misery, self-deprecation, helplessness, and, not least, self-pity. It eventually made for a very remarkable turning point in my learning and living. One aspect of the whole process involved Toni and occurred one day, as I sat close to her in her living room and tears overcame me while talking about this sad event in my life. After a while I looked up. I saw her eyes were somewhat distant, and I became aware that she had been quietly sitting with me in non-dual awareness. This in itself was nothing special or even bad. But I suddenly realized that what I really needed at that moment was a friend who was actively empathizing with my pain, acknowledging that it was true and all right to feel this way. This is not a criticism of Toni or a suggestion of failure on her part, but this was one of the first stirrings of my coming to a different perspective from the one that I had believed in for so long. I had always felt that being in a non-dual state would inevitably take care of everything, but I was becoming more and more observant, practical, and eventually doubtful that what I had believed and had worked so hard for was "the Truth." The importance and complexity of the questions, which developed over time as a consequence of the pain of this separation, demand a bit more detail.

In the late seventies I was living in Cologne with Winston, a lute player, in a narrow "railroad" apartment in an old building without much of a heating system. I had very little money and still had to pay for travel to the U.S. to go to retreats. My only income came from the part-time job making drawings of prehistoric stone tools for a publication of the Department of Archaeology at the University of Cologne. It slowly dawned on me that all the people I knew who were teaching meditation had some money stashed away to fall back on. (Like everyone else I knew, adhering to the original Buddhist attitude, I did not take any salary for leading a retreat or doing any meditation teaching.) Having never earned enough money to save, I was struggling to find a way back into my singing career and became enthralled by the kind of music Winston performed. I formed vague plans to live in Basel—then the mecca of medieval music—and take lessons in medieval fiddle playing, as I had been a violinist when I was younger. I was originally drawn to the viola da gamba, but when my finger tips started to hurt because of the thickness of the strings, I felt it more reasonable to switch to a smaller instrument and one for which I would not have to build up my skill from scratch.

In the early eighties Winston and I were spending a lot of time in Basel and in the summer of 1982 one of Winston's best friends, Ron, a gamba player, drowned while swimming in the Rhine. When the corpse was found someone needed to identify him and I volunteered, knowing that I could probably handle it better than Lena, Ron's girlfriend. Winston decided to come with me and we went together and saw what is rarely seen nowadays, even in films: a drowned body after five days in the water. I could hardly recognize Ron. I was later told by a police officer that bodies taken from the water look worse than almost any other corpses. His body was blown up to bursting and its color had turned dark blue and purple. His tongue, swollen and black, was sticking out of his mouth. At moments like this I could call on what I had learned through the long nights of grueling sitting meditation: to slip into a non-dual awareness when in distress. Right then, therefore, I was not disturbed by the horrible view; as I worded it to myself, it felt as if "nobody was there to get upset." However, I could do it only briefly and the ghastly image nevertheless stayed in my memory for a long time. Winston, with my encouragement, tried to help and spend time with Lena, who was understandably extremely upset. They became lovers and the situation escalated into our very painful separation. I was so preoccupied with my emotional suffering that I nearly caused a serious car accident because of my distraction, not once but twice.

In my earlier years I had always been the one to end a relationship. Now I had been left for another woman, and this triggered strong unconscious childhood anxieties of abandonment, though I did not understand then why this experience was so shattering. Unfortunately, it did not occur to me to undertake any psychotherapy, which would have provided some insight into the deeper cause of my pain. But at the time that was not an option I would consider. I rather believed that meditation and especially the state of non-dual awareness could solve every personal problem.

This difficult period not only meant separating from my lover but also from the music and friends I had found so nourishing, and it lasted about half a year, during which I had to lead several retreats. I did so in spite of feeling very inadequate and almost guilty. How could I take responsibility for all the phrases dripping from my mouth about the stillness of "just being there with what *is*" or the "freedom of boundless love" when I could not master the crisis in my own life? When, at one point, I explained to Toni about feeling a fraud and deceitful, she simply asked, "When a person sits in front of you, or when you give a talk, are you at this moment with your image and your problems, or are you all and everything and empty?"

I replied that during the retreats I would slip in and out of a non-dual state, but was usually quite immersed in it when teaching. "How could I know what I am talking about if I were not in it in the moment?" I said.

She patted my arm and replied, "That's enough. Nobody is in that state all the time and you might learn from this experience and be of help in a more direct way." After that we talked more often about the self-image of being a teacher and its consequences.

I also experienced more of what I had previously noticed, namely, that simply attending to certain basic human needs is sometimes a more effective and yet simpler way of relieving pain and anxiety than withdrawing into a non-dual state of mind. This became clearer and even more obvious to me later through some workshops I took in non-violent communication, where the acknowledgment of these needs was in healthy contrast to my former understanding of "seeing through" them and turning them into peace and quiet. I also remember how once, while alone at a friend's home in Basel, I was overcome with despair about the separation again and was trying to quiet down staring out of the window, when suddenly I was hugged from behind and a soft, flowing fabric was placed around my shoulders and two smiling faces, both good friends of mine, told me they had gotten me a beautiful shawl and I should look in the mirror and see how it suited me. The warmth that emanated from them and their physical embrace I will never forget. It did not remove my pain altogether but it was what I needed in that moment.

It was then that I discovered or perhaps conceptualized for the first time, that being in a non-dual mind state—"dissolving into the Absolute" as I often called it—could in no way be reconciled with a "normal" mind state, even if calm, present, and focused. It was one or the other. Here I was sitting on my cushion in my little room in Basel and could find peace and nobody was suffering; when I stood up, I might be still unruffled but the emotional basis of whatever I was experiencing took over unless I kept the non-dual in place, which then I could not do very extensively when up and about in the world. It therefore became of the utmost importance to find out if it was possible for me to stay in this painless mind state all the time. If not, as I was beginning to suspect, I had to take a hard look at this long training I had undertaken to discover what exactly it was about when viewed not through other people's eyes, concepts, and terms, but solely through my own.

Feeling that I had to extricate myself from the situation and leave Basel, in the fall of 1982 I accepted the invitation of my friend

Phil to live with him in his loft in New York for a while. So I was back in the U.S., where I would stay for a long time, in spite of never feeling quite comfortable in this country.

Chapter 9

Learning to Live

M Y ENSUING LIFE AS A STRUGGLING ARTIST IN NEW YORK was not quite what I had anticipated. Life in Phil's loft in downtown Manhattan was loud, colorful, and cheerful. The only serious problem was the rats, which seemed to have private feuds with each other judging by their battle squeaks and the sound of little feet running at night. The loft was also used for concerts and performances. Having been professionally involved with contemporary music before, I could easily interact with a whole crowd of interesting musicians, composers, performers, and visual artists. I performed my own narrative pieces and participated in performing other composers' music, using violin and voice, both singing and speaking, and I participated also in several avant-garde theater productions. This was the early eighties and it was the time when many people who are now established and famous were part of a big art community brimming with excitement and creativity.

Eventually, to get away from the hustle and bustle of the life in the loft, I got a tiny room nearby at Grand and Lafayette. My doorbell did not work and there was a lot of yelling out of the window and throwing the keys down into the adjacent parking lot with a handkerchief as a guiding parachute. Yet it felt peaceful and was relatively safe, though the city in general felt dangerous and harsh during those years. I had gotten interested in developing a program that I could perform with voice and violin. But I was out many hours of the day, cleaning houses in order to make some money and, over time, it proved too tiring to do both and I let my aspiration to be on stage again drop. Since I had arrived in New York, meditative inquiry had become more of a background hum than an active ingredient in my daily life. I finally realized that, in spite of my sincere yearning to access and stay in a state of non-dual awareness as much as possible during daily living, I was simply swept away by the overwhelming complexity of my many new experiences. Therefore, I was happy and interested to meet with a small group of people who did some kind of meditation in the same building as Phil's loft.

It was there that my life with Bob, who is now my husband, began. We met attending a contemporary dance performance and, since he had been a Zen practitioner, I invited him to come to our meditation group. Yet the excitement of the new relationship and the many challenges it presented somehow made us both drift away from formal meditating. Bob worked in a small photo lab, doing custom black-and-white printing, and photographed performers and musicians for the *New York Times* and other publications, as well as making strikingly intense portraits of many artists and jazz musicians. He was the first close male friend I had had who would stand up to me and not be taken in by my authoritarian manner of expressing myself. For a while, I kept living at Grand Street and went back and forth with my bike to the West Village where Bob lived. Eventually I found some part-time work with a small music publisher, transcribing and laying out scores by contemporary composers. The work was very painstaking and demanding and I cursed America's resistance to metric measurements. Cursing was certainly one thing I learned very well in this environment, and I still remember Bob kicking my shin under the table one day as we were visiting his mother and I remarked fondly that her dinner had been "fucking good."

Finally, we moved together into a tiny flat at Sixth Street in the East Village. With a kind of daily routine setting in, my sense of wondering and inner questioning returned. I took the many opportunities of everyday tasks to dive into inner stillness—going up and down the building's many stairs, brushing my teeth, cutting vegetables, or sitting on the toilet. I also noticed that whenever I felt emotionally aroused, I could seek out this special inner space that I had learned to call non-dual awareness and often I succeeded. However, when I came across the biggest cockroach I had ever seen—with wings and hiding under a potholder—my scream was penetrating and completely unchecked.

Yet day-to-day encounters taught me even more than the insights gained by observing myself or inner stillness. Once, in a hurry as always, I practically bumped into an old man in ragged clothes who held a small cup of coffee in his dirty hand, his fingers almost purple from frostbite. I mumbled my apologies and went on. But somehow he made me think of the envy that was nagging me whenever I heard my rich friend Maggie moaning about the "mere" thirty, forty thousand dollars that she needed to finish an additional part of a film she wanted to put into her performance piece. I wanted to have this problem! But, meeting this street bum, I suddenly became aware how he could think the same way about me. I had a roof, food, a life! How relative our demands and rewards are! As banal as it may sound, I never forgot this moment and kept wondering how much we create our own miseries.

Even so, I had to recognize that I was indeed not making enough money, especially since I had nothing put away in terms of savings and at the time didn't even have health insurance. Something had to change—drastically. Neither house-cleaning nor the job at the music publisher's offered a reliable source of income. I needed to look carefully at what skills I had and how, at the age of forty plus, I could develop them into a profession. Again, therefore, the pressure to develop an adequate plan for survival pushed my interest in finding out more about remaining in a non-dual state in the midst of daily goings-on into the background.

As I got more and more involved in putting together a professional career, however, I was astonished and excited to discover extremely interesting psychological parallels to my meditation training. I had started to take voice lessons again. One of the exercises my teacher gave me made me very curious. While I was singing, I was to rotate one foot to the left and right which made my whole body respond in subtle movement. I asked, "What is this exercise about?" And she answered, "Ah, that's just a Feldenkrais exercise." I wanted to learn more about the Feldenkrais Method.

Moshe Feldenkrais was a physicist who became intensely interested in the relationship between brain function and body movement. He developed a process-oriented learning method that employed specific body exercises as a way of bringing into awareness habitual movement patterns—the way we sit on a chair, how we get into a car, or even how we bend down to pick something up. Consciously attending to these normally unnoticed movements enabled you to change. When I finally did my first workshop with a very accomplished Feldenkrais trainer in Washington, I was thrilled to discover that it was clearly a practical way of applying what Toni and I had been trying to do solely mentally—yet doing something with your entire body is a very effective and sustaining method of learning.

A lesson would always start with several very small movements and develop into one simple coordinated movement of the whole body, such as getting up from a prone position. The final movement would feel easy and sometimes unfamiliar because it used new groupings and sequences of muscle action. After a lesson in "Awareness Through Movement," I often learned something valuable, without knowing beforehand what it would be, and I discovered how, in a very physical sense, learning can take place without a fixed goal. I also observed the now familiar pattern of my trying to do too much, too fast, and too willfully to observe the full range of possibilities this situation of subtle movements offered. The process also showed how evaluating the quality of an action may be totally justified but usually goes together with feeling unworthy (or proud, which produces the same vulnerability), and is not helpful to a situation. Staying attentive during movement, attending to the quality of what I was doing without the typical inner judgment, was truly refreshing and really another form of meditation.

Soon after I discovered the Feldenkrais Method, I visited my cousin Jutta in Germany. She lived with her family in the caretaker's house of a castle on top of a hill in the middle of fields and woods with only a few other houses nearby. One day, when I gave her a glowing report of my new discovery of the Feldenkrais movements, she remarked that this reminded her of the crazy singers in her neighborhood who would sometimes sing while balancing on a bar or do scales while jumping on a trampoline. This piqued my curiosity, and thus I discovered what would be the second big influence on my budding career as a voice teacher.

A group of experimental voice teachers had formed the Institute for Functional Voice Training. They were mostly interested in investigating the anatomical and physiological transactions involved in singing and had developed a teaching method which took account of the laws they had discovered, applying a process-oriented approach to learning that was similar to the Feldenkrais Method. The dominant idea was not to develop a preconceived sound but for the voice to emerge solely through doing specific exercises, based on a solid physiological understanding of vocal cord activity. I started to take lessons and courses and became an enthusiastic follower of the method. It was not until a few years later that I realized I had fallen again into the trap of exclusiveness.

Yet the studies they had done and the theories they had developed provided me with the means to follow my goal of building a professional career, especially when I discovered a way to get a valuable degree. I needed a recognized qualification and was searching for a way to get a degree of some kind that would include the many skills I had accumulated. This proved to be difficult and elusive until I met Paul in New York. He asked me to be his guinea pig in testing a seemingly esoteric body-mind educational method he was learning. I remember lying on a massage table, with Paul holding my leg and moving it very, very gently backward and forth. His touch was like a breeze and I remarked how unusual it felt and how much I liked it, but wondered how effective it would be. He smiled—my response being exactly what he was learning to address in his future clients—and said, "So, tell me, how would you talk to your leg, if you wanted it to do this movement?" I had to giggle. "Hmm, yeah, I would probably scream at it: Get in line! Do your thing!" We both laughed and again I had come across my habit of harsh will and controlled inner discipline. What Paul had demonstrated was actually part of the Feldenkrais Method called "Functional Integration," which I had not been exposed to yet and involved physical manipulation by a practitioner. What was most interesting was that Paul had done this training as part of his Master's degree program with Antioch University, which did not require you to take prescribed courses or be physically present at the school. What sounded like heaven opening its doors to me turned out to be quite demanding.

Pursuing my studies meant attending the Institute for Functional Voice Training in Germany and, in 1987, Bob and I decided to move to Cologne. I had to take a number of Functional Voice lessons and also to sit in on the lessons of teachers at the Institute and observe their methods. The foremost thing I learned during these many hours was that it is not enough just to know a method; what is really crucial is knowing how and when to apply it. I also had to confront my ever-active nemesis, my will to control. When practicing my own voice, my habitual forceful attitude conflicted with the proper way of producing a head voice, which, in its essence, is the most effortless way of moving the vocal cords. Generally it is most desirable to use head voice and chest voice in an integrated way, to produce a sound that is flexible in volume but not pressured. Because of my willful personality, I was using the cords with much more pressure than necessary and therefore restricting their movement. To be confronted yet again with the same traits that I had struggled with in meditation practice and that had made me unhappy so often was very frustrating and challenging. And, as I discovered, switching into a non-dual mind state did not automatically erase physical habituation. Since addressing habitual movement patterns and changing them was the particular strength of the Feldenkrais Method, for my thesis I developed a parallel training structure for voice teaching and started to use and refine it as soon as I began teaching.

In general, my meditation practice and the resulting psychological insights were of great value and played a big role in my effectiveness as a voice teacher. I also think that my success, not just in facilitating better singing and speech skills, but in creating mutual warmth and respect, had to do with giving suggestions, corrections, and evaluations without threatening my students' self-esteem. Nevertheless, I believe that, without having learned and internalized so much about the physiology and anatomy of voice production, I would never have been able to successfully apply the many different methods and approaches to voice and speech development or to discern who needed which one and when. I also noticed that when teaching speech or voice I was clearly in a kind of "flow" that permitted creativity and sensibility and was not ruled by an ego-driven need to succeed.[9] Yet this state of intense but non-compulsive involvement was distinct from being in a non-dual state.

By the time I had finished my degree program, Bob had decided to further his education as well and do an MFA in Rochester, and therefore we moved to upstate New York. I could not believe that I was relocating to exactly the city where I had spent many years of Zen training and had wandered forlornly, wondering where the actual "city" was. Now, almost twenty years later, I was confronted with my own history and given the opportunity to look afresh at what was not really "Rochester" but a memory, a succession of emotionally charged images and would, therefore, perhaps be able to discover a new kind of city and a habitat for a different life. And so it was. I started to give voice lessons and travelled to Germany, working as a speech coach for stretches of six to eight weeks at the National Theater in Mannheim, as well as other theaters in several cities in German-speaking Europe. I also held workshops and gave lectures about combining the Feldenkrais Method with my approach to voice teaching at several highly regarded conferences. When my many travels permitted, I would sometimes participate in meditation sessions with some of Toni's students living in Rochester. I enjoyed being with them, without any specific tasks or ties to the Springwater Center. Bob and I made the best of the somewhat limited possibilities that the area offered our passion for hiking, given that the summers where bug-ridden, very hot, and humid, and the winters dumped incredible amounts of "lake effect" snow on us. We found a bike path along the canal and sometimes went to the Lake Ontario shore. Bob's personal photography there caught the sensuous stillness of our human surrender to the timeless, intricately wordless quality of nature.

After Bob had finished his coursework, he applied for and received a research fellowship at the National Gallery of Canada in Ottawa. So north we moved with our cat, furniture, and my newly acquired headaches which turned out to be migraines. We had learned that it would be easier for me to immigrate to Canada as Bob's wife and so we took the opportunity to marry, after having been together seven years, which made both our mothers happy. When Bob's fellowship came to an end, he returned to the Rochester area to finish his thesis on a highly regarded but little-known photographer. We also realized that we had to begin to earn money, not only enough to live on, but also enough to pay back our student loans, and decided that I would try to find employment in Europe, where I had better chances, having already worked there a great deal.

Chapter 10

Interlude in Munich

S OON AFTER I SPREAD THE WORD THAT I WANTED TO STAY IN Europe and was looking for a job, I was offered a position as a speech trainer in the theater department at the Bruckner Conservatory in Linz. Bob agreed to move to Munich—Linz, a small provincial city, was not feasible—and I started to commute. I was now 50 years old and for the first time had full-time and steady employment. As I became intensely involved in mastering a completely new situation, my quest to increase non-dual awareness in daily life lost prominence. In fact I learned a great deal about myself and changed my perception of the world through ordinary everyday experiences.

Aside from teaching at the Conservatory in Linz, I started to give private voice lessons in Munich. One of my students was Lilly, living with her husband and two enchanting children on the outskirts of Munich. They allowed me to use their garden house as my studio, and I kept using their facilities for many years while teaching in Munich, even after I had moved away. Living with this family exposed me to cultural values that were different from those I had held so far and had never questioned.

I was a whole-hearted non-believer in astrology. Lilly, on the other hand, immediately after we met, asked for my birth date, drew up a chart, and deduced my character, difficulties and psychological obstacles with hearty conviction. While I inwardly scoffed at this, I also remembered an incident that I had completely forgotten until then. A long time before, on a Tuesday in 1965, I had stood under the shower in a hotel room in Manhattan, getting ready for a performance at the Carnegie Recital Hall. At 5:27 I reached out with my wet hand to turn the light on and, as I touched the switch, all the lights went out in our hotel room and, for that matter, in the hallway as well. The phone didn't work either. I was mortified. I had caused a short circuit for the whole building. Of course, we later learned that I had not personally brought about one of the biggest blackouts in New York's history. In this case I was glad to be proven wrong. Nevertheless, seeing Lilly's involvement in something that I regarded as pure fantasy, I now realized how little all of us need in order to assert causes and effects or propose relationships, and most of the time we are not even concerned about proving whether our conclusions have any basis in fact at all.

Another challenge to my convictions came from the serious involvement of Lilly and her family in Sufi meditation. I once asked Lilly what her ultimate goal in meditating was and, after a short pause, she answered, "ecstasy." Being trained originally in Zen this was not part of my spiritual vocabulary, nor was believing in God, as Sufi doctrine, based in Islam, did. Yet, through my friendship with Lilly and some other members of the same spiritual community whom I greatly appreciated, I realized with greater clarity than ever that my own psychological and philosophical framework was nothing absolute. I also became convinced, however, that believing in a dualistic worldview—a God, a higher consciousness, or some other kind of spiritual truth—is probably not something we choose. Rather, it is probably part of humanity's characteristic makeup, whether genetic, developed in our earliest childhood, or both. Through the earnestness and love with which my hosts and friends attended to decorating their home in a style unappealing to my taste, to sports which I was not interested it, to esoteric practices which I did not believe in, and to many other aspects of their life that to me felt completely unfamiliar, I slowly learned to see through their eyes and appreciate their delight in so many things I had initially found unattractive and pointless. And although I could never adopt the same views, this understanding of the relativity of my own viewpoint contributed to the constructivist worldview that I later developed more fully.

After almost two years of pursuing promising projects that failed to produce satisfying results, Bob decided to go back to New York, expecting to find a better chance of suitable work in his field there. In late August of 1995, Bob and I flew to New York and spent the summer together. Then I went back to Munich and my job at the Conservatory in Linz, and Bob remained in New York.

Chapter 11

Learning to Differentiate

COMING BACK TO EUROPE ALONE AND LOOKING AT THE empty walls where Bob's photographs had hung, I felt no need to stay in Munich any longer and moved to Linz. I had developed high blood pressure and had to take regular medication and began to exercise. Long walks, often in non-dual awareness, became the equivalent of formal sitting meditation. Walking without a center, without a "me" from which to look and smell, and with no associations springing forth, was the best way of relaxing my body and mind. The landscape surrounding Linz is hilly, lightly forested, and with many small traditional rural homes like toy houses strewn over the green hillsides. It was, and still is, a relatively poor area, especially compared to the heavily traveled tourist landscapes around Salzburg or the Alpine ski areas. In the fall, I would choose specific paths that were lined with apple and plum trees and collect the fallen fruits. I often had quite a bag full of harvested goods to carry home and enjoy. I loved the rich, dark brown earth of the fields in spring and the sugar-dusting of a light snow crust in winter. It was here, in an environment of intense work but also of intense aloneness, that I discovered more about the puzzle of living with a brain condition that I had once learned to call and think of as "enlightenment."

One day, on my way home after a heavy work day, I was feeling exhausted but relaxed and content, a mind state that was not guarded.

I was walking through a small park with wonderful old trees and small groups of bushes when I felt as if I was walking through an atmosphere of what I could not conceptualize as other than "pure love." I had had similar experiences in the past, but never of such intensity. I was overwhelmed with joy and elation. This feeling of love was certainly not directional, neither towards something outside nor *towards* myself inside, not towards anything, since there was no center from which it came. Yet as I was describing this experience to myself I was bound to call upon the language which I had learned to use in this context.

Following this thought, I became curious about how the language and style of Toni's teaching had evolved, and I occasionally flew to Springwater to attend retreats. Toni often changed verbal images. For example, she used the word "awaring" for being in a state of non-dual awareness while sensing the environment. She also used the word "seeing" for the same mind state and "not knowing"; perhaps influenced by her immersion in the teachings of the Indian Advaita[10] master Nisargadatta. I also became interested in his ideas and read his books and found a very different language from the one Krishnamurti used, which no longer resonated with me. I read: "The real world is beyond the mind's ken; we see it through the net...of our desires, divided into pleasure and pain.... To see the universe as it is, you must...see your net as made of such contradictions and remove them—your very seeing them will make them go."[11] The proclamation that the "seeing" will solve the very problems of our personal involvement is repeated in many ways and by many spiritual teachers, including my friend Toni. But was it true? Or was it the language that suggested the effects.

I started testing what problems could indeed be addressed by a non-dual awareness. On the outskirts of Linz, I had found a very skilled dentist who practiced his craft with the dedication of a medieval book illustrator. He convinced me that I needed to get rid of all four of my wisdom teeth, though, he conceded, not all at once. Sitting in his waiting room I felt quite nervous about the forthcoming operation and, because of the discomfort this feeling brought on, I almost automatically switched into a non-dual state: my vision broadened and my anxiety vanished instantly...until a moment later I was called in and tensed up again and everything was as before. But I tried again and noticed how relaxed my hands, my breathing, my jaw could become as long as I remained in this mind state. So I started to experiment with this situation. After a few attempts at declining the anesthesia—very much to my dentist's displeasure—I gave up. I couldn't hold on to the non-dual mind state, and the resulting imperturbability, once the pain became very strong. So I decided to accept the anesthesia and try focusing on the *expectation* of pain, which I still felt despite the injection. Now I could observe clearly how this tension disappeared upon switching into a non-dual awareness. Equally clear was a situation when I was sitting in a car with a good friend who had the same meditation background. We were waiting at a river crossing for a drawbridge to come down. I had sighed somewhat impatiently, and he had smiled and remarked, "We really can't do anything about it, can we?" At this moment I experienced an internal change and all impatience subsided. I had shifted into non-dual awareness. So I asked him curiously, "Where do you think your patience right now came from: the reasonable deduction you just made or from switching into non-dual awareness?" He answered quickly, "From the reasoning, of course!" Then he paused, hesitated, and continued, "No, it actually comes from the openness, the complete letting go! It's a different mind state than just being reasonable." It seemed non-dual awareness would change my perception and therefore perhaps influence my attitude towards a situation, but did it affect my behavior?

Sometimes transformations of behavior did occur. Once, while standing in line at a bank in Vienna, a rather portly gentleman brusquely cut in front of me. Immediately I thought, should I just be patient—easily done by sliding into a non-dual awareness—or "work" on my feelings of intimidation and fear of rejection? Gathering my courage, I said, "Sir, would you mind staying in line. I was already here before you." He turned, completely failing to comprehend what I was saying. "What? What are you saying?" My heart sank. "You just stepped in front of me. I have been waiting in this line for quite a while." He looked at me with the kind of expression reserved for cockroaches. "So? You'll get your money exchanged in time. What else do you want?" He turned away. This was not meant as a question. I took a deep breath and stepped forward catching his eyes. "I would like you to realize that being big, male, and perhaps rich does not give you the right to do what you want, including being extremely impolite." He just snorted and turned around. I was exhilarated. I had opened my mouth and behaved against my conditioning. It simply felt good, no matter what the outcome.

The teachings I had been exposed to had showed me that in my case feeling timid in social interactions was a form of ego—wanting to be loved, admired, not rejected. By being attentive to these normally unconscious feelings and thoughts, I slowly learned to detect and dissolve them. How much was this change in my behavior caused by non-dual awareness? I had to admit: not at all. Obviously there were situations in which I benefited greatly from psychological insight obtained through the philosophical framework of my meditation practice, but that had nothing to do with a direct implementation of a non-dual mind state.

Then there were other situations, where I gained insight into peculiar and unnecessary traits of mine but couldn't change them. Influenced by my several sources of spiritual teachings, I had learned that identity was nothing but the expression of a form of attachment and quite unnecessary. In this light I had discovered that language played a much bigger role in my own constant process of asserting who I was than I had initially thought. I became aware that my German accent in American English was not due to ineptness of ear or tongue, but rather to my subconscious distaste for certain sounds which were typical of American pronunciation. Although non-dual awareness provided me with short moments of equanimity, this insight did not motivate me enough to change.

Observing what this differentiation meant in my own daily living, I noticed that there were always these two basic possibilities: simply gaining insights by observing the impulses which made me act or shifting into non-dual awareness. I seemed to use a mixed approach. In difficult situations I alternated, often rapidly, between switching into non-dual awareness to gain some distance from my rampaging emotions and then, after calming down, reflecting on the role of my self-image, the way I had learned to do through meditative inquiry.

So, was I the only person who could not wipe out habitual and damaging traits by just "seeing through" them, implementing non-dual awareness? What was the true relationship between non-dual awareness and teaching meditative inquiry, which provided guidance for becoming alert to the emotional and psychological aspects of daily living? Could it be that the language, the conceptualization of non-dual awareness, influences what is taught more than the actual mind state? Although these questions started to hover in my mind, a dramatic challenge was needed to shake me out of the notion that I knew what I was doing when I taught meditation.

Chapter 12

Interlude with Myself

LTHOUGH MY REGULAR AND INTENSE INVOLVEMENT WITH meditation while living in Linz initiated reflections on what teaching meditation meant, the foremost events in my spiritual life were of a different nature. I began to experience a shift in the nature of the episodes of non-dual states. It is difficult to say with certainty what brought about this change. I didn't own a television and in the evenings, when at home, I would read or listen to music. By this time I more and more felt the need just to sit on my sofa doing nothing, moving in and out of non-dual awareness, experiencing what seemed to me an increasingly profound grasp of this mind state. Looking back I now believe that this was at least in part due to my renewed and intense involvement with the writings and teachings of several meditation teachers.

Because of my high regard for Nisargadatta, I was especially interested in several Advaita teachers and became quite immersed in their specific language with respect to non-dual awareness. I was also impressed with a little book that Toni had read by a woman who had contacted her but had died before they had the chance to meet. Her name was Suzanne Segal and the book was called *Collision with the Infinite*.[12] I was awed by her account of non-dual experience, because it seemed permanent for a while, but I was also confused, since she was besieged by attacks of fear when in this state.

Another strong influence was A. H. Almaas.[13] His short account of the several non-dual mind states he describes in his book *Luminous Night's Journal* fascinated me.[14]

I found my greater ability to access non-dual awareness voluntarily and the concurrent expansion of its dimensions difficult to describe with any accuracy. As we live, we "make sense" of what our inner and outer experiencing provides. It seemed I only knew that a non-dual mind state was present when I recognized it as such, just as experiencing a headache has to be in some way conceptualized to come to my attention. Like most people who meditate, I was still not aware that—whatever my experience—it was inevitable that my specific interpretation of it would be through a received religious or philosophical theory. I had read beforehand what to expect, so I had a preset description for the event. This is not to deny the experience of a truly different kind of awareness, but, as we conceptualize that awareness to ourselves, we do so in accordance with our memory, training, and expectations.

I tried to write about my experiences. However, as I had yet not realized the extent to which I conceptualized or interpreted what was going on in my brain and body, my notes most certainly reflect the concepts with which I made sense of what otherwise would probably have been fleeting unremembered moments. Then I was still convinced that there was something universal and somehow other than mere brain activity going on: an all-embracing consciousness already in place into which we sort of immerse ourselves. In other words, I still shared the notion that this mind state was a manifestation of absolute truth.

In early February 1998, I wrote:

"…*Sitting quietly yesterday something profound, yet silent, dark, but not threatening, emerged.*"

"…I realize now that I don't need practice or anything like 'sitting'…"

"…this all-embracing state is so much clearer now. It doesn't seem difficult to project thought without losing that deep, pervading presence."

"…I can talk on the phone—there is talking but nothing is done. It feels like a child playing with incredible energy, laughter, and joy."

"…It's not empty. It's whatever it is."

"Total unconcern. Total completeness. Perhaps not so different from before, just more inclusive, more on a daily basis?"

"…Still my question is: How do I live out of this openness in all my activities?"

"…I keep asking myself: Shouldn't there be 'love pouring out of me?'… but in living there can't be love constantly. There can be openness to everything. Maybe that in itself is an aspect of love."

"…I am so full of joy. Sometimes there is fear of losing this fullness of life. Yet—why should there be uninterrupted joy all the time? Why should anything be all the time?"

"…I guess, somehow the Absolute, in order to experience itself, has to go through the process of becoming conscious… Is that true? It is all still so fresh. I need to keep everything as a question."

"…this morning doing my callisthenics. Hating it. Then switch— and nothing anymore. Just doing it. No emotion."

Further notes, later in February and during March, read as follows:

"… There is no self. Still I feel something different than simple awareness of sensing. Something deeper (what exactly does deep mean? Somehow this seems to be a meaningless comment)—a silence, a quietness…imperturbable."

"… Today I saw clearly: There is no like or dislike when acting out of silence—but it doesn't mean there is no thinking. This way more energy is available."

"…a horrible day. Completely dominated by my discursive mind. After a long time of sitting and 'awaring,' slowly a gentle flame of the quiet liveliness reappears."

"…next morning waking up into a wide void."

"Noticing how frantically I wanted to be 'open,' 'loving'… without any 'burden.' Realizing that it is no problem being quite normal and 'closed' when I don't see it as wrong."

"…sometimes I am dark, focused, concentrated pointedness, sometimes wide, wide openness, sometimes blinding brilliance…"

Reading these notes again I can see clearly how I used concepts and descriptions that at that time were relevant to me. I also understand how the concept of "mysticism" has evolved. These utterances would all sound pretty mysterious to me as well if I could not connect the words to my actual experience. Yet why should anyone need to call upon anything supernatural or divine when reading or hearing about an experience that they somehow simply haven't come across yet? If I had been able to describe these events differently, would they cease to sound so mysterious? Eventually I would reach very clear explanations about this and the many questions that had evolved during my investigations. Yet, at that time, I was too excited about my increased ability to stay in a broad and seemingly solid state of non-dual awareness to follow this train of thought. Toni was cutting back on her travels in Europe and asked me to take over some of her retreat work load again. Sustained by the knowledge that I could experience non-dual states more frequently and at will, it was perhaps only natural that I became more involved in teaching and tried to do my best to motivate and guide people's interest towards their own experience of non-dual awareness.

Chapter 13

The Turning Point

SOME SIMPLE WORDS OF PRAISE FROM MY PILATES TEACHER A few years ago—when I was in the role of student—and the effect they had on me made me think again about the teacher-student relationship in the context of spiritual practice. I was always very aware of the possibility for dependency in a teacher-student relationship and this was an issue of some concern to me. Viewing the teacher as superior seems especially to be one of the prerequisites for forming a dependent relationship and students often project superiority onto their spiritual teacher. I remember sitting on a bench on the outskirts of Linz with Helga, a former acting student of mine, when a class of little schoolboys approached, happily babbling and milling about. As soon as our bench came in sight a big flock of them ran towards us and all tried to settle on the side where I sat, practically crawling all over me. About ten minutes later, after the boys had left, an elderly lady came along with a little dog by her side. All of a sudden, it took off and tried to jump into my lap, or at least onto the part of the bench where I sat. Helga was dumbfounded. She knew I was leading meditation retreats and started to utter things like, "They sense you have a special aura…" and so on. I got pretty angry with her, but also tried to make her aware of how we are prone to establish connections and project causes and effects randomly if we are not careful. "What if my side of the bench smelled better to the dog?" "Or perhaps the boys just followed one who hadn't even looked where he was running!" Do we, as people, really need so strongly to project greatness, superiority, something more than what we see ourselves as being, onto somebody else or, for that matter, onto an omnipotent entity? It is an old question, but it was part of the reason why I felt, over the years, that I had to look more closely into what I was doing when leading retreats or when serving as a spiritual teacher.

At one point, when Toni and I had spoken about the danger of students channelling their projection onto either of us as an "evolved" human being or somebody "who knows," Toni had concluded by saying, "Let them do what can't be avoided. But I have nothing to teach." However, in the kind of meditative inquiry which I had trained in and which I had assisted Toni in developing, I had always felt that the role of the teacher was somewhat ambiguous. I understood her stance but was never quite satisfied with it. I felt, for example, that if I sat on a chair surrounded by people quietly listening, while only I spoke for an hour every day for a whole week (as is done in a retreat), what could anyone expect? I remember when Toni was quietly walking through a room of people meditating and then stood for a while behind an individual, some people remarked that they felt "blessed" or overcome with love when she stood behind them. I decided that I had to think of myself as a teacher and therefore be clear as to what exactly I was teaching and where that emanated from.

In 1998 I had resumed leading retreats in Poland and at Roseburg, a Buddhist retreat house situated in a beautiful landscape near Hamburg in Germany. I was also invited to lead retreats at the Tildeberg meditation center in the Netherlands. These retreats were mostly an opportunity for long hours of sitting meditation, but people were free to walk wherever and whenever they wanted as long as silence was maintained within the retreat grounds. In addition to a teacher's talk in the morning, we also offered private meetings with the teacher. Later group meetings were added, replacing some of the private meetings. I also felt compelled to open the floor to questions after my talk. This was a structure that I felt comfortable with in the context of my understanding of the role of the teacher.

At the time I was convinced that experiencing a non-dual mind state would bring improvement to our personalities or to our life, and serve as a basis for changes in attitudes and behavior. In our style of teaching we did not promote specific rules of conduct, and it had become Toni's style—and later also that of most of her successors—to make suggestions in the form of a question. This would leave more room for the individual to bring up an inner response, but it might also coax the person into an inquisitive, curious mind state. I used the word curiosity a lot, since it seemed for me the best way to depict the innocence, the unbiased possibility, of inquiry. When teaching, I often used the image of a little puppy which is picked up from one place and put down somewhere else. It doesn't hang on to where it was but promptly starts sniffing and is freshly excited about its discoveries. This was an image which, many years later, I recognized as one of the many that had been a handy teaching tool but did not necessarily hold up well in real life, especially not in mine.

At the start of a retreat, I would address how everybody's allotted tasks were typically performed. I pointed out how we habitually judge everything we do either from an idealized standpoint—*I should not think, I should be attentive*—or from a self-centered one—*I'm bored with this, I'm annoyed by what I have to do*—and how these emotions, when unobserved, set a general mood and prevent the opportunity for waking up to the "actual moment." I recall saying, "Boredom is not possible when you are truly awake to the living moment as it is." Often I used what presented itself at that moment, asking, "When sitting quietly on your cushion or on your chair, you look a lot at the floor. Have you ever really looked at the floor? Can you look at the floor not with your eyes, not knowing what it is? Can you stay baffled for a moment? Really try? Can you look at the floor without the mind?" Sometimes I would pick up seemingly unrelated subjects like language and show how even abstract words like "understanding" have their roots in the senses or in actions connected to the senses. I felt that the senses were in general the strongest tool for a person to use in order to disrupt the constant flow of thoughts and emotions. I would say, "Even the weight of the body when sitting can be felt; there is the light in front of the eyes, the birds twitter—none of this needs to exclude any other." Or I might ask, "Can you sit at the table and chew with all your heart and taste with all your heart and be so busy tasting that you forget to tell yourself what it is you are eating?" "When holding a broom, drying a plate, walking in the grass, can you stay with your hands touching the broom, the weight of the plate in your hands, the smell of the grass? Each moment is filled with myriads of non-verbal information and excitement when we don't *know* what we hear, smell, feel—when we are so close, so intimate with it that there is no space for a word or definition."

In my talks I sometimes addressed the attitudes and emotional reactions that accompany how you listen to a person—constantly judging the relationship that goes with it, needing to protect one's beliefs. I would suggest to the listeners that they perhaps observe the hurt they felt when their efforts might not have been recognized or if they were held responsible for something they had no hand in. I devoted a lot of time to examples of using hurt or anger as an opportunity to find out about hidden motives or fears. Often I used my own life to illustrate what I was getting at. For instance, I would describe my feelings when a voice student told me excitedly how she had found out about a "new approach" through a workshop she had just attended, when I had been teaching and saying exactly the same to her for years. I would propose that all of these reactions could be resolved by plunging into "a moment of no interference of the mind whatsoever," a moment of stillness and inner listening. I would not give advice about how to act in given situations, but rather emphasize that a moment of stillness would lead to a proper response.

I was also acutely aware how a teacher could and needed to influence the atmosphere and energy in the meditation hall, not only by the content of the talks, but also by the manner in which the talks were presented. I often drew attention to sounds from outside to get students to pause and listen, inviting stillness while listening, and sometimes I reflected on subjects which had come up in personal meetings. Off and on, I used relatively coarse language and at times quite unflattering examples of failures in my own life as an intuitive means of counteracting notions of superiority. Yet sometimes I felt it was important to lighten the mood and I would insert silly scenes as an example for serious subjects: "We are often not aware how much every moment of our life is dominated by expectation. For example, at a busy train station we may unconsciously divide people into travelers and those waiting for someone to arrive, just from judging their behavior and appearance. If somebody was standing there, holding a red rose in his hand, we might only become aware of our hidden expectation if he suddenly started eating the petals of his rose."

Like many other meditation teachers, I had to come to grips with the fact that we couldn't function without thinking, in spite of the implications of enlightenment's being something beyond thinking. Therefore, I would make the distinction between functional thinking and "wandering" thoughts. The first would do the job of helping the organism to get sanely and smoothly through life and the other would interfere with assessing and responding to a situation unencumbered by its habit of dreaming up images and scenarios. I spoke of a "spontaneous" and a "compulsive" way of acting: one is in touch with "reality," the other comes out of memory and projections. Yet it was exactly these two concepts, reality and the complex nature of memory, that I felt compelled to examine in depth later in my life.

Another frequent subject of my talks was fear and the different sources of angst or anxiety. Though I would admit that there was no courage without fear (otherwise we would not have survived as a species), I would invite my listeners to investigate the different situations in which we could discover how fear can dominate actions. "Whether it is hidden or open, fear of losing our dignity or the love of another person may be the reason we act aggressively." Sentences like this were meant to cause a moment of pause and reflection when such feelings emerged. But, ultimately, they were uttered in the belief that, as the listener could switch into a non-dual mind state at a moment of distress, the emotion in question would evaporate, thus permitting action free from a fear-driven motive. During a retreat in Poland, when I had gone for a little walk, I had a very interesting encounter with a more concrete form of fear. Walking along a deserted road, I had to pass between two dogs sitting in front of their respective gates and one of them started to growl quite menacingly. I had always been very fond of dogs and was normally not afraid of them. But it felt unwise to not heed his threatening demeanor. Yet I also thought that it was an interesting situation and I wanted to find out if I could stay in non-dual awareness when passing between them. I kept closer to the lazy, friendly-looking one, and I did indeed run this gauntlet, more or less staying in a fearless mind state. The seemingly aggressive dog had not advanced any further and I was safely on the other side. Was this a stupid game? Was I proud? I don't remember, but I think it was then that I started to wonder what was happening in my brain when I was doing this. Where in my brain had the fear stopped existing? Was it gone simply because I didn't feel the equivalent of its physiological expression? Was I still emitting something chemical that dogs could smell as fear, or perhaps not? Would the dogs have picked up on that? What was going on when I lost the sense of fear?

An encounter like this during a retreat was just a short moment in what was usually a series of quiet, though very intense, days, mostly occupied by my endeavour to teach how to trust this strange, vibrant silence, a silence deepening and swallowing even the slightest notion of emotional upheaval. Sometimes I simply would ask, "Knowing what you see in front of you is a way of controlling what will happen in the next moment. Here we are safe, at least for the next five minutes. Can you just for a little while trust your breath so completely that you forget to label what you see? Can breathing BE you? See with your breath, hear with your breath? (a long pause) What is seeing or listening when we are so intimate with it that we are not observing it anymore?" As I was listening to tapes of my talks, I smiled when, during the long pauses, I could hear a symphony of bird chatter, which I had enjoyed then as well.

Another subject that I would investigate step by step was how we develop guilt and how it is usually connected to our self-image (today I would perhaps say to our super-ego). I would clarify how our concern for our self-image thoroughly prevents our ability to empathize truly with a person we feel guilty toward and may therefore prevent us from responding constructively and from allowing us to let go of a mistake. The examples or subjects that I talked about were also meant to be vehicles to evoke a moment of stillness. Whenever I spoke about anger, guilt, fear, boredom or anxiety, I would ask, "In the midst of turmoil, can there be a short pause, a back-pedaling, a moment of awareness in which we allow ourselves a kind of vulnerability, a helplessness? Can we ever be completely clueless about everything at once?" Aside from the really big issues like death or love I would mostly address the daily possibilities of "practicing." I stressed that staying focused on what's in front of us, on a moment of seeing that "in reality there was only stillness," would lead to becoming aware of our inner commentaries and dissolving them instantly through the understanding that there is no need for self-image and its confabulations. I would make suggestions of how to be completely involved with all the senses without the inner dialogue—when brushing teeth, using the toilet, climbing stairs, starting a car, locking a door, or even looking into the mirror first thing in the morning.

In private meetings people would bring up questions that were often quite personal.

As a meditation teacher, I was not, however, concerned with the personal aspects of the problem but rather with taking the question and using it as a means to bring about a moment of stillness and, if possible, of non-dual awareness. Once I encouraged a woman who had come with a complaint about feeling lonely and depressed to sit for a while quietly, not pushing those feelings away. After a while I asked her to touch her skirt with her breath. It was the right moment for this kind of seemingly confusing request. Her eyes widened and she tried to talk but couldn't find words. Then I could tell that she had stumbled into a non-dual experience. Finally, I smiled and said, "It's easy, isn't it?"

But some subjects that were brought up led to more analytical dialog. For example, responding to the question of whether it is possible to repress unwanted emotions by replacing them with the calmness of non-dual awareness, I usually acknowledged that this is feasible but is only useful if one is aware of doing so and doing so for a good reason. I stressed the importance of non-judgmental inquiry, of allowing the free flow of emotion and, at the same time, of questioning why these specific emotions were being rejected. In severe circumstances, I even recommended consultating a psychotherapist.

Generally the concepts I used were completely in line with those of many other meditation teachers. Yet, as I kept doing this work, I started to question what exactly made me competent to offer such statements and utterances. It also became more and more of a burden for me to dig into my own life in order to come up with what I thought would be authentic and lively teaching. Then in the summer of 2001, while leading a retreat at a Buddhist center in Poland that our meditation group had rented, I finally came face to face with my doubts. Every morning, more people were joining our little core group for my talks, as they were open to everyone including, of course, our hosts, and I could see people with Buddhist robes and other visitors standing along the wall, since there was no more space for mats or chairs. At the conclusion of one of my talks, I was asked a seemingly innocent question, "Are there facts?" I replied without hesitation, "Of course there are facts—or have you never cut yourself with a knife? But from an absolute point of view there are no facts. You will have to experience that in order to understand."

The answer I had given had been within the standard range of answers that address the possibility of an absolute standpoint, one that is experienced as having no standpoint at all. However, by the end of this retreat I knew I would not teach meditation again until I had found out once and for all why I was saying what I was saying. Why should my insights be more valid than anybody else's? I had always referred to my words as not coming from "me" but out of "silence." Yet the silence or emptiness from which I— and other meditation teachers—proclaimed the words of wisdom to be emerging was…silent.[15] Nevertheless, when this silence was present, words and concepts and images still flowed easily. How was this possible? Where did they really come from? How could I or, for that matter, anybody talk reasonably out of an awareness in which there are no concepts whatsoever and no center from which to speak? I realized it was not enough for me any longer to call talking about non-dual awareness "witnessing," as was often done. For the next several years, therefore, my unease with the given explanations, which had been growing for a long time, increasingly became a motivation and desire to *understand* this kind of awareness— what many sources called "enlightenment"—much as my original yearning had been to experience this mind state. Only this time I would not only observe but also read and learn about what generally was called "consciousness."

Chapter 14

Learning to Think

WHEN I WAS SEVEN YEARS OLD, I STARTED TO ATTEND the children's service at the Protestant church that my mother was a member of. Every Sunday morning I heard stories about this wonderful person called Jesus, who was so kind and had to suffer so much. I learned that he was the son of God and I already knew *him* well because I had prayed to him every evening since I could remember. I always felt totally blissful and protected when the minister, toward the end of the service, opened his arms wide, held them high up in the air, and announced that God, his son and a ghost (which I could not make much sense of, but one that I knew was special and not bad) would look after me, bless, and protect me. When my mother was very ill and lying in a hospital, I would walk home from visiting her, praying for her recovery intensely with all my heart. Soon, I would feel warmth spreading from deep down in my belly, making me calm and quiet. It was perhaps five years later, as I walked along the same street that a thought struck me: When I had walked this street praying, would it have been different if I had prayed to Allah? Would that have worked too? If I had grown up in a country like India, who would I have prayed to? Obviously I was never short of questions. Some of the "answers" I had gained through my involvement with meditation made it possible for me to speak and teach with conviction and trust about non-dual awareness. They had been answers about the very nature of who I am and what is real and what is illusory. But now I was not so sure any more and was wondering how I had come to believe in these concepts. I could not doubt my experiences, but I started to question what I had made them into.

When I read again what once had been precious sources of inspiration and guidance, I started to understand why it is so difficult to untangle the many different components that contribute to our beliefs and convictions. I re-examined my earlier reading and it seemed to match my own observations, but I now realized that my understanding was in a sense predetermined by the concepts I had read and heard. I had always found some convincing bits of information and I had unquestioningly accepted the way that these were packaged and offered. I found that many spiritual teachers, as I myself had done, mix and freely stir all kinds of concepts—borrowed from psychology, art, and science—with great impact on how the students experience and understand the teachings. But do these teachers realize that, in their endeavor to facilitate the experience of enlightenment, they are offering pedagogical stepping stones, interpretations from their own experience, creating an entire conceptual framework around that experience? I hadn't. Not only had my almost lifelong relationship with Toni made her someone whom I trusted completely when she said that just "seeing" (being in non-dual awareness) was enough and took care of whatever was happening in the moment, but I had also been exposed to innumerable other sources of distinctive advice, descriptions, and proclamations about non-dual awareness and what it takes to attain it. Amongst them all, I had probably accepted utterances that made me feel a little uneasy at times, because they did not seem right—just like you overlook disturbing features in a person you have just fallen in love with.

Here are a few examples. Aside from the general doctrines of Buddhism, which I had soaked up in my Zen training,[16] there was Nisargadatta, whom I had always loved for his stunning way of expressing ideas. He wrote: "it is Consciousness—the manifested objective aspect of the unmanifested Absolute—in which appears the entire universe, including the millions of human beings." Once I had swallowed this, right along with everything else he said. Now I was asking: How does he know this? And his former pupil R. S. Balsekar talks about non-dual awareness as having "no solidity at all" and compares it to his understanding of particle physics: "The compact nucleus at the very heart of the atom, then, is nothing solid at all but rather a dynamic individual pattern of concentrated energy throbbing and vibrating at an incredible speed."[17] In a general sense this is very compelling, and I had always found remarks like these totally enthralling and taken them as a proof of what non-dual awareness must be. However, I now felt a little uneasy when philosophical or psychological discourses took a cherry-picking approach to science, while at the same time condemning the scientific attitude in general as belonging to the world of illusion. Also later, when I listened to lectures about quantum mechanics, I understood that many phenomena—though very tempting to take as metaphor—occur under very specific circumstances and do not apply to most normal scientific measuring results, let alone the average person's day-to-day experience. Similarly Eckhart Tolle, one of the most famous teachers to expound a wisdom that has no specific lineage and one whom I had admired, compares our "normal state of consciousness" with a "continuous low background noise, which we can only feel when it suddenly stops as a sense of relief..."[18] and he also states that "your perception of the world is a reflection of your state of consciousness. You are not separate from it, and there is no objective world out there." A statement like this builds up trust, since most people who experience non-dual awareness would not deny that this concept is a reasonable philosophical, if not scientific, statement that expresses the experience of a non-dual state. Yet he too could not resist the lure of modern physics. He goes on: "the person conducting the experiment—the observing consciousness—cannot be separated from the observed phenomena, and a different way of looking causes the observed phenomena to behave differently."[19]

The confusion that I felt many teachings caused were the seemingly obvious truths they proclaim, mixed with what I could see now as personal opinions and individual worldviews. But, since these rather personal statements came within such convincing generalities, I had not given specific scrutiny to them but rather taken many utterances for granted. For example, Tolle refers to the "pain-body," which we can transform into radiant consciousness by applying complete attention. Addressing women specifically he states: "Menstruation will then become not only a joyful and fulfilling expression of your womanhood but also a sacred time of transmutation, when you give birth to a new consciousness."[20] Now, reading it again, it left me speechless. Why would anyone who seems to be able to witness—he calls it the "watcher"—a non-dual mind state refer so explicitly to specific situations, explanations, and solutions? Not that this might not be helpful, but what does it have to do with a non-dual consciousness? How come all these teachers seem so convinced that what they say is anything other than their personal story *about* a mind-state—one about which all *I* could say is that it is completely quiet? The question here is not the teachers' integrity, but why and how they come to these conclusions.

When Jiddhu Krishnamurti spoke about our "conditioning"[21] and how it misleads us into identification with our beliefs, he implies that there is an unconditioned state of mind. This seems to suggest the possibility of an unconditioned way of living, a supposition I also came to question. How can we make any decisions, write e-mails, hold conversations without our conditioned understanding of the specific environment we are acting in? Perhaps what he meant is that we should frequently observe and *change* our conditioning if it seems useless? But why didn't he say that? Also, after having listened to many of Krishnamurti's conversations with David Bohm when I was still very enchanted with Krishnamurti, I began to read Bohm's book *Thought as a System* again.[22] Here too I found what I had once thought of as an interesting, insightful remark. Bohm writes that thought is not "proprioceptive,"[23] meaning we don't feel a physical response emanating from what we think, as opposed to the joints in our body which provide feedback about our movement; it is therefore very difficult to become aware of it. This observation reminded me of the long and difficult process of learning to be conscious of the movements of the tongue when singing, precisely because the tongue also has no proprioceptive capacity. However, now, after further reflection, Bohm's argument didn't hold up so well. Was I not experiencing physical responses to thought when quietly observing and differentiating how emotions and thoughts correlated?

When I further investigated the original sources of my spiritual language, I found more examples of how personal interpretation of non-dual experience was used in a pedagogical setting. There were the writings of Ramana Maharshi,[24] one of the most lucid meditation teachers and a beacon of his tradition, who had been one of my deepest inspirational sources, especially early on when I was still struggling with my koan. I had taken very seriously for a time his suggestion of preparing for death as a means of letting go of the ego and his attitude of "surrender." His simple admonishment "be still" had carried enormous power for me. The attitude of "surrender" was taken further and made even more personal by another teacher of this line, Gangaji: "Absolute freedom is untouched by relative freedom or relative bondage, and you are That.... just surrender to That."[25] At the time, this had made perfect sense. Again I did not question that this might have been a helpful psychological tool, but was she aware that it was no more than that?

Another instance of this mixing of insightful observation and unsubstantiated generalization caught my attention when I reread Jack Kornfeld's *After the Ecstasy the Laundry*. This book can be enormously helpful with mindfulness meditation, helping to slow down and observe habitual thought-emotion interaction. Yet when I read in this very same book how Kornfeld cites the Buddha advising us to look at what is "wise and healthy...independent of any text or teaching or authority,"[26] I was puzzled. First, because of the contradiction of quoting an authority in order to admonish the reader not to do so and, second, by the tacit understanding that this citation seems to imply, namely, that we have some inner moral judgment per se independent of learning and experience.[27]

Obviously when people are dedicated and very seriously involved in a meditation training, they often go through an intensive process of change. Meditation teachers therefore apply a great deal of motivational and stimulating skill to shaping their beliefs, reconditioning assumptions about themselves and the meaning of life. I now believed that this process was wrongly attributed to the experience of the state of non-dual awareness itself rather than actually being based on a specific *interpretation* of this mind state. It seemed to me that what is so gracefully called "waking up" to non-dual awareness—or whatever expression is provided—is actually waking up to a preconceived knowledge of a description or concept that fits into the experience. This explains why insights, or even changes in behavior, are prompted by the concepts that are internalized about the experience, rather than through the actual non-dual awareness itself.

Later, in a workshop about non-duality, I was told that, through awakening to a non-dual awareness, my ordinary self had been transformed into an "Authentic Self." In the past, this would have impressed me very much, because the teacher heading this workshop was a neuroscientist, who had done interesting scientific work on so-called intrinsic and extrinsic networks of the brain.[28] But, by the time I participated in this workshop, I no longer allowed myself to confuse my respect for his professional work with his spiritual teaching. I finally understood that this statement was nothing but a personal interpretation of an experience and that I did not even know whether it resembled what I would call non-dual awareness.

When I was wondering why it had taken me so long to kickstart my critical thinking, I found a possible reason from my training as a musician. As a spiritual teacher, my training in my meditation tradition had been much like the transmission of the tradition of music or art or a craft. You soak up the principles and skill of teaching by going through the process of your own learning for a long time without much of an analytical attitude towards the sources. This might explain why, for so many people who are deeply involved in the practice of their respective spiritual tradition, no questions about its validity ever arise. It is almost like the concrete learning we do as small children through interacting with our environment. The basic beliefs we develop during meditation training are equally difficult to examine, especially when they get reinforced by our own and other teachers' statements. I too, as a student, had unconsciously projected my own experience onto the language that I encountered. I now understood how I had taken interpretations, personal opinions, and my own mix of language and concepts about non-dual awareness for granted.

Chapter 15

A Conclusion

I T WAS CLEARLY TIME FOR ME TO GET SOME PERSPECTIVE ON THE particular role that non-dual awareness played in my life. Recalling and investigating unpleasant situations helped me greatly in developing and honing a conclusion.

Three examples:

In addition to my teaching position at the conservatory in Linz, I had taken on an additional part-time teaching job at the University for Music and Performing Arts in Vienna, and I therefore commuted between the two cities. I took the train in the morning and came home, exhausted, late in the evening. Yet I loved the train rides, the landscape going by with its familiar but ever-changing features: the collection of snow on the windswept hills, the lonely little church tower peeking out of a flat grassy meadow. My love for public transport, though, was always put into check by late and crowded trains and by standing and waiting in cold winds, rain, or heat. Often being besieged by a horde of teenagers pouring into my train compartment, chattering at the top of their lungs, with earphones emanating scratchy sounds, would bring me to the verge of tears or blind rage. I wanted to slap their mouths shut, stamp on their headphones, and push them out of the compartment. Unable to do this, I often did finally remember to switch into a non-dual state. And there it was: The instant this mind state established itself, all emotional upheaval completely vanished—though it took a bit longer for my whole body to gain its equilibrium. And then, after a substantial pause from my emotions, I was able to figure out a strategy about how to deal properly with the situation.

There was also the repeated ordeal of flying to and from the United States—sometimes four times a year. The crowdedness in the plane, my inability to fall asleep with the back pain that would inevitably appear after an hour of sitting in the narrow seat, possibly with a corpulent neighbour, all made me highly agitated, and I often started to cry silently. There was nothing I could do. With the realization of this helplessness I would finally wake up, remembering I had a choice. I switched into a non-dual state: my tears instantly stopped and my agony and hostility vanished. Or, as I put it to myself for a long time: There was nobody there anymore. Again, after having quieted down through non-dual awareness, I was able to cope with the fact that I could not change anything in this situation other than my attitude about it.

A more complex situation occurred after I was invited to join the faculty of Vienna's music university full time, which entailed my moving to Vienna. I was living in a beautiful apartment in a restored Biedermeier building with a courtyard that was home to an ancient mulberry tree. I missed Bob. I wanted to tell him about my new friends and my new environment. Fortunately, overseas calls had become cheaper and Bob and I started to phone each other more frequently. I could voluntarily switch into non-dual awareness while talking to him, but I would never notice the moment when I slipped out of it. It was not only curiosity which prompted me to do this. I was struggling with the notion of attachment to Bob, which I felt made me vulnerable and unclear in my words and actions. Whether this struggle was still left over from my Buddhist training or my ceaseless need for security, I don't know. I just remember that one day, a few years later, I realized that the very nature of our relationship was based on attachment and, if I was afraid of that, I should not be involved in it or, for that matter, in any enterprise which needed motivation and investment. Yet, during an argument, I was sometimes able to switch into non-dual awareness. It created a kind of mental space and I could try to assess what was going on without immediately spitting out words that would hurt him now and me later. But during this resulting "calm" mind-state, with my body still slightly agitated with the chemistry of angry arousal, I often felt quite helpless and without any insight as to how to proceed next.

Over and over, whenever it came to the actual non-dual mind state, I was left with the same conclusion: shifting into non-dual awareness would always remove emotional involvement and give rise to an experience of perception without a perceiver. But it would not provide me with instructions, knowledge, or guidance for acting or understanding what was best or most appropriate for a given situation. I was left with the fact that solutions and reactions would have to develop from my own personal resources as well as my biographical and genetic background.

This meant that non-dual awareness was a perfect help in any circumstances where I couldn't do anything about the situation, and it would assist me when struggling with blindly driving emotions and confused mind states. However, it could and would never tell me what is right or wrong. And it certainly couldn't provide me with motivational input to do something. It functioned as a unique support system within the context of the discursive mind or, perhaps more precisely, the educated self-consciousness, balancing drive and reason.

Therefore, I was now convinced that this specific kind of awareness was a mind state that happens through specific physiological circumstances and that it can also be trained like so many other features that the brain is capable of organizing. Like sleeping, dreaming, or ordinary wakefulness, non-dual awareness (a non-intentional, strictly non-relational, attention), is not common but obviously possible and can exist parallel to a normal consciousness. This conclusion did not negate or take away from the significance of the quiet peace and mental space this mind state provides and which, left to itself, is without the need to be explained or identified. What I had gradually come to suspect now seemed evident: There was no grand super-consciousness that includes or gives rise to the "puny mind." No absolute truth with a capital T. Of course, I could still envision this specific awareness as a manifestation of a universal consciousness that permeates all and includes all and was timeless and somehow "always there," positing that normal consciousness was just a deviation from an everlasting Oneness (the non-dual awareness), existing even when not noticed. Yet how would one know something is "still" there if one wasn't aware of it? It seemed so much more plausible to see non-dual awareness as a specific network of neural constellations switching in and out of play, instead of inventing a "continuous" timeless (non)-entity. Understanding non-duality as a function of my brain seemed to me the least contradictory of all the models and worldviews I had come across that try to conceptualize this special kind of awareness.

I wanted very much to discuss these ideas with other people who had had similar experiences. But I was afraid they might say that I didn't know what I was talking about. And how *would* we know whether we were talking about the same experience and mind state? What was the raw experience behind the words? Finding out what was going on anatomically and physiologically in my brain while in a state of non-dual awareness looked increasingly like a reasonable path to follow. It seemed equivalent to my experience as a voice teacher. Understanding the physiological processes involved in voice production had been important in helping me to differentiate pedagogical constructs from physical facts. Then the language and concepts with which I was struggling wouldn't matter. For that, I had to discover if there were neurological attributes of this mind state which could be tested in order to correlate personal impressions and judgments with physiological activities. I had to find out if I could come up with precise physical data.

Chapter 16

Portrait of a Mind-State

I FIRST CONSIDERED THE NOTION OF PHYSICAL PROOF FOR A NON-dual state when remembering the time I had accidently cut my finger with a Cuisinart during my early years at the Zen Center. There had been a first moment of complete shock, in which nobody was there to "tell" me that I had cut myself. Then, after a fraction of a second, I seemed to split up into somebody—a *me*—and something that was recognized as pain and with it came the agony of *me* feeling *it*. In a non-dual mind state no division of this kind exists. There is pain but somehow it does not bother me, as if nobody is there to feel it. I would especially appreciate this ability when I had to get through a seemingly endless session of cardiovascular workout. As long as I was in this state of mind, there would be no temptation or inner debate about giving up before the exercise was finished. This clearly was not the same as being distracted from pain by reading or watching a video to "get away from it." I began to wonder if perhaps participating in a research project that dealt with the cognition of pain could shed some light on the biological factors of this specific awareness.

I also noticed that in a non-dual state I did not differentiate sensations into separate perceptions. When perceiving a sound, or tasting a fruit, or smelling the ocean, I would not connect these sensations to my ears or my mouth or my nose, or for that matter to my body at all. Sensations in general would not elicit any reaction when in a non-dual mind state. For example, sudden loud noises didn't have a startling effect, though sometimes the body might react, but with no conscious feeling of shock.

I thought that what is often called "emptiness" in accounts about experiencing enlightenment is more what I would now attribute not only to the elimination of concepts but especially to the absence of emotional reactions. This was even truer in the case of smells. Mild scents would easily stay "empty," though especially unpleasant smells often would force me to revert to a normal consciousness. Fascinated by the ability to eliminate emotional responses to sensation, I tried touching my own feces, something that would normally be quite revolting for me to do. This indeed proved possible without a trace of repulsion when in non-dual awareness. The ability would disappear as soon as the non-dual state was off. This was, therefore, apparently very different from becoming inured like nurses or a parent changing baby diapers.

Another subject that I found worth exploring was the notion of having no body, in a literal sense, while in a non-dual state. But how come I could still walk, hold a spoon, or blow my nose? How could I move at all while my "experience" told me that instead of a body there was nothing? How could this be investigated? There was nobody I knew to whom I could talk to about all this. One day this conundrum became clearer while taking a qigong class. I was practicing the exercises in non-dual awareness and, given my feeling of emptiness instead of a body, I did not know how to deal with the teacher's advice that I should pay attention to my spine. Only when I realized that I could simply imagine my spine and still be in non-dual awareness could I complete the movement. It seems that we form an inner body image in order to consciously know what we are doing. Somehow, like breathing, the body image is something which happens involuntarily and voluntarily as well. In fact, I later learned that there was a well-established differentiation between a conscious and unconscious body-mapping in the brain, which was referred to as body image versus body schema. Obviously my body schema was always working but, through non-dual awareness, I seemed to deactivate my body-image. This explained to me why I could do exercises when in non-dual awareness yet feeling as if moving without a body. It also became clear why in this mind state I could touch my knee, but have no awareness that it was part of my body, or why I did not even feel a difference between my arm resting on a table and the table itself. Could this difference in self-perception be tested?

I also asked myself how this notion of a physical body image was related to the psychological notion of "self-image." Because of my training in the Feldenkrais Method, I was aware that a huge part of our psychological self-image develops through our body image. I remembered one peculiar incident in this context. It occurred during a Feldenkrais lesson I gave to a voice student in Boston. She came to me because she needed more flexibility in her jaw in order to use her voice properly. By the end of the lesson she could open her mouth so wide that it prompted her to remark that she felt "not quite herself." I should have listened then and not gone so far in my lesson as to allow such a sudden and extreme change. The next morning she called me, mumbling quite panicky, "I can hardly get any food in my mouth. What is happening? What did you do?" I was terribly embarrassed and felt very sorry for what she was experiencing. I calmed her down and told her that she would probably be alright by the next day and that her nervous system was just overreacting to the strong deviation from its self-identity. It was very obvious that the many moments of her experiencing the limitation in jaw movement had solidified in somatic patterns and formed an aspect of her psychological self-image. Was there a psychological self-image when in non-dual awareness?

I remembered reading about tests that had been done with animals looking into a mirror in which some would recognize themselves while others wouldn't. When I looked into the mirror while in non-dual awareness, the person looking back at me was of no significance. It was not a foreigner but it was also not "me." Stated differently, the mirror image looking back at me did not evoke any reactions. Then when switching back into normal awareness, I became "me"—with a pimple on my forehead I didn't like and wrinkles that I didn't like either. Switching back again to the non-dual state, the pimple stayed, but didn't stick out particularly and the feeling of dislike was gone. (When had I learned to dislike pimples?)

An even more obvious self-image connected with my body-image arose when dressing, whether in my imagination or actually doing so. In a non-dual state I would not have any judgment or opinion about what suited me. Nevertheless, as soon as I reverted to a normal mind state I could be upset if a haircut was bad or elated if my new summer dress gave a boost to my self-image. Another interesting aspect was that, when in non-dual awareness, I was neither embarrassed nor nervous in front of a camera. And when looking at photographs of myself I felt no connection with these pictures, but only as long as I was in non-dual state. As soon as I reverted to a normal mind state, my criteria of how I preferred to look would usually take over. Perhaps these clear differences between being in and out of non-dual awareness were a promising path of inquiry.

In a non-dual mind state every moment is unconnected, that is, if there are even such things as "moments" when there is no concept of "now." There is no notion of time and space. Since music is structurally based on time, I found that when listening to music, I would hear clearly but no musical line would develop, no sequence, no repetition, no emotion. When listening to a car-siren going by, I did not automatically attribute it to a sound moving in space. Another change in perception of space appeared when I was walking along a ridge in the Alps and was afraid of looking down. This unease disappeared completely when I switched into a non-dual awareness.

As I had already ascertained, emotional components of perception didn't exist when in an non-dual state. Equally, all emotions related to time and space ceased, such as impatience, boredom, or reacting to cramped rooms. And, just as I had noticed at the dentist in connection with the anticipation of pain, I experienced the same lack of anticipation when interacting with space. When I crossed a room with my eyes closed, I would feel a certain tension in my body, just because there was a chance that I would hit something. When I switched into non-dual awareness the tension vanished, although nothing else was different. I would still walk carefully and bump or not bump into something on the way.

Yet I still could not define why I could sometimes stay in non-dual awareness and why at others I would shift back involuntarily to a normal state of consciousness. It was clear that emotional participation would end the non-dual state. Talking seemed possible, as long as I stayed either with the subject of non-duality itself or with accounts that did not involve explicit emotional values.

One day a partial answer emerged. When I was walking through my living room dusting and cleaning, I bent down and picked up a little scrap of paper that was shining white on my dark-colored carpet. The strange thing was that I had been in a non-dual mind state. How come that I noticed the paper scrap as special? In non-dual state there were no differentiations, no "things," and certainly no irritation. I had experienced this over and over. How come I reacted to this trigger? Perhaps I had slipped out of non-dual and then back in? And then I remembered that I could wash dishes, take a shower, brush my shoes…do most of my daily chores while in this mind state, just as I had been able to do with my exercises. There was no emotional involvement. This mind state could run parallel with anything I did, performing a whole program of habitual tasks, as long as they were done automatically. It seemed that I was able to do a lot of activities that are normally seen as needing discrimination and a subject-object-driven mind state. Obviously I was using a specific set of memories related to habitual tasks, without self-conscious supervision—very much like the situation with the body schema and the body image. I was glad about this clarification, but I was also aware that I probably wouldn't be able to find physiological verification since this implied a very complex test situation.

Summing up my observations, I compiled a list with the most prominent characteristics I thought would be useful for testing and showed them to a few friends, including Toni, who mostly agreed with the attributes I had registered. Although the list draws together many of the features that I have already mentioned, it offers a succinct summary:

- Loss of body image. No sensation of "inside" and "outside," no experience of body boundaries. Pain is not "seated in the body," it does not evoke a localization. It is possible to reestablish the body image, but without a specific "this-is-me" feeling

- Timelessness. A clear perception of "being without time" or "outside of time." No expectation. No impatience.

- Normal perception of space ceases. (For example, no direction is evoked while perceiving sound.)

- Comparative judgments, whether perceptual, emotional, or moral, are suspended. There is also no frame of reference, no point of view in a psychological sense.

- Open attention. The mind is not focused on anything. (In my personal experience there is no difference whether the eyes are closed or open.) There are no associations and no emotional reactions. Hearing, smell, sight, taste, and touch are not experienced as belonging to different categories, and they are experienced simultaneously and with equal intensity. Differences are felt but not conceptualized. No specific location within the body is assigned to individual sensory events. There is no habituation to repeated sounds; also, a sudden loud noise will not trigger shock reactions (in some cases the body may react, but no "shock" is felt).

• Inner and outer sensory perceptions (hunger, thirst, pain, itching, etc.) are not felt as "I am experiencing that."

• Absence of a conscious emotional component. Perceptions, mental images, and actions are experienced with no emotional content.

• Accessing concepts is possible. Memory, including biographical memory, perception, and action are experienced as empty of personal meaning and are not part of, or in any way connected to, the non-dual awareness.

• Cognitive learning so far has not been possible. Learning motor tasks by imitation or verbal instruction seems possible, but needs further exploration.

Some people missed any mention of compassion and universal love in my compilation. I certainly had experienced these emotions at times, but they were not features that were present automatically when in non-dual awareness, though I certainly could evoke and personify what felt as a loving kindness in this state. I realized that I had done this a lot when I was teaching meditation. It made for a caring, though impersonal, attitude towards whoever sat in front of me and often, mixed into the feeling of love, was a notion of respect for the participants of a retreat. Sometimes it felt as if I was embracing and being embraced all at once. Often there was also a gentle, joyful peace while sitting or walking quietly in this mind state, which somehow didn't feel emotional.

I also needed to clarify my use of language. Since it so strongly affects and structures how we conceptualize our experience, this is not an insignificant issue. I was quite aware that I was using language the way we normally do, which reflects a dualistic worldview of subject and object, when saying that I *was in* non-dual awareness. This did not mean in any real sense that there was a personal me that was in this mind-state or that I was entering something, but simply reflected that communicating through normal language—as this book also does—involves inevitable compromises and metaphors.

Now I was ready to move on with enthusiasm to find places to get tested, unaware that there were quite a few surprises to come.

Chapter 17

Brainstorm

THE EXTENT OF MY NAIVETY WHEN I STARTED TO PURSUE the task of finding opportunities to get scientifically tested relates back to an event that took place in the early summer of 1995. I was attending a symposium on the Feldenkrais Method and had listened to Francisco Varela giving a talk on the nature of perception.[29] He was one of the most prominent scientists studying the relationship of Buddhist philosophy and cognitive psychology.[30] At breakfast the next morning I told him I had been involved in meditation for a long time and that I was interested in the brain and how it might be involved in this kind of mental activity. As I started to describe attributes of a non-dual mind state, he interrupted me with the question, "What initial training have you taken?" I told him that I had done roughly ten years of intense Zen training before moving on to a mindfulness type of meditative inquiry. After I explained to him about my attempts to find out more about the nature of non-dual awareness he seemed quite satisfied and invited me to join a group of Tibetan lamas in southern France he was working with, experimenting with a brain imaging set-up he had developed in Paris. I was not at the time aware of the rarity or the exclusiveness of an invitation like this. I rather felt I did not want to be involved in another Buddhist-related context, so politely declined. It was only later that I learned how highly regarded he was in the scientific community and the likelihood that so much more would have come from his research had he not died so early. Coming back to the subject almost ten years later, in carefully compiling my observations about non-dual awareness, I learned that the best-known research about meditation was performed in association with the Mind and Life Institute, a collaboration between western scientists and the Dalai Lama, that Varela had helped to initiate.[31]

Realizing that so much research was centered on Tibetan Buddhist meditation, I recalled a conversation with a dear friend of mine. She had advanced breast cancer and was a mature Tibetan meditation practitioner. I learned from her that in Tibetan Buddhist terminology *rigpa* stood for "the open state" or "clear light" awareness that seemed very similar to non-dual awareness. Especially interesting for me was a remark of hers about the fear of dying that would overwhelm her sometimes when she felt her body withering away. I asked her, rather timidly, since I didn't know if I could do this myself in her circumstances, "Don't you slip into the 'open state' when you feel this way—wouldn't that relieve your fear?" She replied without hesitation, "Of course! It would and it does… but it does not stay." Since her experience and what I had read so far seemed close to my own experience of non-dual awareness, I wrote to one of the researchers involved in meditation research with Tibetan Buddhist monks[32] about this similarity. In my note, I asked if they were planning any tests on these subjects. In his reply he cautioned me about my comparison, mentioning that we know too little yet to be able to compare different trainings and results. I also learned that for most of the tests only highly experienced Tibetan monks and lamas were asked to participate. Later, when I knew more about the very specific types of meditation that were measured, I could only agree with that decision.

In my eagerness to get tested I made a connection with one of the cognitive science labs at the University of Vienna. So one morning

I walked into the office of one of the leading scientists there and pressed my list with the phenomena of non-dual awareness into his hand and asked if he thought that the manifestation of a specific "me" feeling was due to having emotions. Reading through my list he looked at me with mild...was it concern or interest? Somewhat carefully, he said, "I don't think so. But we can put you on a waiting list for some of our pain endurance evaluation tests, if you want." I sighed—I wanted. I never heard from him. Similarly futile were my attempts to work with a young researcher at the Eberhard Karls University in Tübingen and with many other labs.

Not being part of the scientific community or involved in the field as an academic made my attempts to connect to a scientific lab extremely difficult. Because of my work schedule, I was not able to attend most of the relevant conferences, and this was clearly a handicap. All of this left me feeling frustrated and like a weird creature who did not fit in anywhere. I was desperate and decided that I had to study the relevant scientific literature about consciousness, no matter how difficult it would be for someone who had an extremely limited knowledge of the anatomy of the brain and of the functioning of the nervous system.

At first, I relied on reading the books that were featured in an article in a *Newsweek* magazine. The headline, "Religion and the Brain," seemed to promise insight into the physiological nature of non-dual awareness. Yet most of the publications and books referred to in this article, though appearing at first very promising, disappointed me. Religious interpretations of test findings were mixed indiscriminately with biological data. Most of the time, the religious context of the cases that were discussed was never questioned. My discontent was aroused most prominently by the substantial book *Zen and the Brain* by the Zen Buddhist and neurologist James Austin, since his neurological investigations where based on an unquestioned Zen interpretation of non-dual awareness.[33] He, for example, described his *kensho* experience, which happened while he was standing on the platform of a train station in London, as one where "instantly, the entire view acquires three qualities: Absolute Reality, Intrinsic Rightness, Ultimate Perfection."[34] I could only wonder how these very specific conceptual terms came so precisely to describe for him this non-conceptual, non-verbal experience. The book also contained so much information about the chemistry and physiology of the brain that at times it became overwhelming and confusing to a lay person like me. However, I did find some ideas and phrases that seemed to fit with my experience, as when he explained the expression "no mind" in Zen with the phrases "bare attention still registers percepts" and "there are no emotional reverberations."[35]

After spending almost all my free time buried under heaps of books and with my nose pressed against the computer, I came up with some understanding of how my brain functions with regard to keeping me conscious and attentive. It was exciting and rewarding to learn how intricately complicated and complex the simplest act of any sensory recognition is. Neurons talk incessantly with each other (though not all at once) and the brain (engaged almost entirely with itself) does an incredible amount of neural communication to create the sight, smell, and taste of something that my memory than accepts as, and what my language system calls, a strawberry. More and more, I began to see the networking of the brain very much like a constant mini-evolution: each neuron, neuronal ensemble, or momentarily unified network is competing to "come through" and to be dominant, and is counterbalanced by other neural, electrical, and chemical forces to inhibit these events.

I became especially alert when I learned that, in order to elicit actions, agreements seemed necessary between certain neuronal hubs and evaluation systems like the limbic system or the frontal cortex. Yet I still did not know exactly what had happened in my brain when, for example, in Poland I had walked fearlessly between those threatening dogs by switching into non-dual awareness. It was clear that I didn't know enough. I found the closest thing to an explanation for non-dual awareness in general in a theory by the neuroscientist Gerald M. Edelman about something he terms "primary consciousness." He refers to it as a "remembered present" that is self-aware but does not construct a "socially defined self" or a biographical self.[36] Equally promising were Antonio Damasio's books,[37] alluding to a self that is reconstructing itself perpetually, and *Being No One* by Thomas Metzinger, a philosopher who connected his theories closely to neuro-scientific findings.[38] Yet, none of what I read explained the cessation of emotion that I experienced.

Though starting to understand a little bit more about my functioning as a biological entity, I became increasingly dissatisfied. I felt more and more in a haze. Why did I need so desperately to know exactly what was going on in my brain when in non-dual awareness? Why was it so important to learn what I was sensing? The real explanation came suddenly and was painful. One evening when I was rummaging through a box, looking for a notebook, I came across a cutting from a newspaper. I looked at it and broke into tears. It showed the photograph of a scrawny little cat sitting on the tracks of a subway station in New York. The caption described how this animal had made its home in this environment and was surviving. So far it had refused, with all its puny might, to be taken away and ignored food offered by passengers. I was stricken. Why was I sobbing? I let it go, but the same thing happened every time I looked at the picture. It was as if all the loneliness in the world descended on me when looking at this little cat. Then one day, sitting at the wooden desk in my bedroom, I looked through the windows, which were densely framed by dark green vine leaves clinging to the walls of the building. My view wandered to the swaying branches of the old mulberry tree, some purple berries still visible, and—the change was instant—the light intensified, colors were pristine...with no limits, no direction from which this was seen, or heard, or sensed. THIS was the reason I was doing all this. Falling into or accessing a mind state that was not shared by everybody else and that was barely describable was strange, to say the least. I realized that since I had left the shared ground of spiritual interpretation of non-dual awareness and, with it, all the emotional and conceptual backup for living with it, I was alone with my observations. I was no longer part of the bonding that is such an important part of the psychological support and orientation when establishing new experiences. Whenever I had participated in a retreat, it had provided new confirmation of being part of a community, validating what it was that I encountered.[39] I had very consciously given that up, to find out how to come to grips with the many contradictions I had discovered within the various systems I had trained in. Was it worth it? Somehow, realizing and accepting how lonely and vulnerable I was, had a healing quality. I did move on—gently and more humble. But I kept going.

Eventually, from all my reading I understood how difficult and multi-layered this direction of research had become.[40] Consciousness research is a field that is drawing on philosophical, psychological, and biological investigations. I had given up the Buddhist understanding of the world and myself as pure illusion and reality as something beyond our perceptive abilities. I couldn't buy into that any more. Nevertheless, here I was, experiencing—at least sometimes—the world and myself as completely without substance. Yet, during most of my daily life, the world did not feel illusory but very real and full of consequences. Whatever understanding I had gained through my research into the biological factors of consciousness had not brought me closer to integrating these two seemingly conflicting experiences.

Chapter 18

In Fact...

W HEN I STARTED TO TAKE DRIVING LESSONS, MY TEACHER would frequently yell, "Red! The color red—ever heard of that? It means to step on your brake!" Was seeing the color red real and my experience of non-dual aware-ness—where no color was named or conceptualized—not? Or was it the other way around, as Buddhism claims, the red traffic light was an illusion and my perception of "nothing" was real?

Through my investigation into neuro-scientific explanations of exactly such events I was intrigued to learn that, in distinguishing a green or red traffic light, our brain not only fabricates these colors through an emergent pattern of neural activity, but for finer differ-entiation of colors, like orange and brown, additional cognitive sub-networks are engaged that have to do with language and culture.[41] My husband and I are mutually amused about our inability to agree on the color of a certain overcoat, which I call green and he laughs and says, "but it is brown, can't you tell?" Is what we each individu-ally experience indeed reality, or have we simply learned to differ-entiate and name a sensory experience that is relatively similar in all human animals?[42]

Here, I felt, was a lead that would help me to make sense of my contradictory types of awareness. I discovered that in the uterus we already hear, feel, sense and, through likes and dislikes, we form non-verbal concepts of experiencing our environment. Is not this the basis of what we later refer to as reality? Wouldn't a little dolphin embryo develop quite a different reality? Studies dealing with babies in their first year of life show that, as soon as their senses can differentiate their surroundings, they start putting order into their experiences by categorizing what they come into contact with. Already at the age of seven months infants, their visual system finally in place, seem to expect even a stuffed animal to move on its own but not a ball.[43] This would mean they are able not only to categorize—recognizing an animal as such—but also to generalize that living things move on their own and objects don't. It is now widely believed that many basic traits, which we formerly assumed were learned, seem to be wired in the brain and happen without verbalization. The baby, waving its hands from side to side, grasping, finding its mouth, may develop a "doer," an agent that acts and is separate from its action but connected, a self, and therefore a perspective, all through neuronal networks that translate as space.

We make sense and attribute relevance by acting and moving. One could say by "doing" we create what we think is a continuous reality; it is even argued that without constantly moving our eyes we wouldn't see anything.[44] In other words, we form specific concepts, concepts that fit our evolutionary background. We couldn't—as perhaps our four-legged friends would—create the concept of a corner that smells enticingly like female urine. It would seem that any living creature, with a similar brain, investigating its environment early on through its senses, would develop similar sets of categories and concepts and so experience as real what its brain has created.

I finally came across an account likening our experiencing of the world to walking blind through a big forest, never able to see where we are. Wouldn't we learn about "our world" by walking, moving one way or other, experiencing the spaces between the tree trunks and touching, smelling, remembering, and imagining? Wouldn't we develop and share intricate inner maps of our environment and a viable knowledge of what we consider our surroundings, without ever knowing what's "really" out there? We can only rely on what our specific human cognitive enactive brain provides us with, and it is a brain that does not seem to be able to develop without its environment.

My research had led me to the idea of constructivism,[45] which seems to provide a convincing explanatory model of how I could relate what I feel to be real and normal living to my equally strong experiencing of nothingness. Now I could explain both non-dual awareness and what seems to be factual reality as very elaborate constructs of my brain. I did not need the reference to either the concept of illusion or to an opposing reality. What I call real is a useful concept within a specific relational framework and therefore not an absolute term. I no longer have to pose the question of the existence of anything absolute—it would only be another self-created concept.[46]

I feel alive, experiencing and learning, without ever knowing what reality "really" is; in fact, reality is an invention of this very construct—me—though this "I" may deny being just that. Nevertheless, just as Newton's laws are not proven wrong by the discovery of quantum mechanics, so my personal world is not invalidated by knowing that I have created it through my specific way of experiencing. The capacity to discern the relativity of all laws doesn't make them unnecessary or invalid. Constructivism basically says that, regardless of our efforts, we can never have absolute knowledge.

For me, realizing the transience of my seemingly solid environment means acknowledging that I am always bound to have a subjective standpoint, though this doesn't mean that the relativity that ensues from it is arbitrary. We live within a complex system of cultural and socio-cognitive learning. We have basic assumptions, the sources of which we are mostly unaware of. This makes it even more necessary to question what I feel to be a hundred percent certain. In a constructivist view, we determine facts by developing models and explanations that we test and prove—this includes the willingness to change one's assumptions when proven wrong. Given that my experiences and memories constantly create what feels like a continuous "me," it is not surprising that this identity is challenged and threatened when assumptions and convictions are questioned. After all, any belief or conviction is connected to learning, memory, and the subjective experience of a collective. Non-dual awareness may help me to observe how I cling to my conclusions, how the capacity for modifying or relinquishing a conviction disappears when great emotional value is attached, turning it into a belief, a "Truth."

The idea of a purposeless self-generated universe, constructed by brain cells is an incredibly humbling yet comforting basis for living, and it forces me to respect other beliefs and viewpoints at a very profound level. I may stand up for what I think is better than something else, but it doesn't automatically lead me to vilify other beings who think differently.

I finally made peace with the seeming contradiction of being somebody and nobody. Yet, in my daily living, more often than not, I still came head to head with the grinding insistence of improbable personal responses and reactions that were not changing for the better, no matter how much clearer my understanding of the world and its governing laws were, or how often or intensely I experienced non-dual awareness. Why? This question became even more pertinent when, with the onset of post-menopausal hormone changes, half a lifetime of suffering from debilitating migraines came to an end. This was a surprise, after I had gone through years of extensive, yet completely fruitless, therapies. Later, I took artificial hormones because they were the only way of alleviating extreme sweating and the terrifying moments of misery, despair, and suicidal intentions, just before the onset of the actual hot flashes. Hormones—how much am I the product of chemistry? Even simpler: How does the physical state of the body influence decisions? Don't we tend to react differently when needing to go to the bathroom or not having slept enough...not to mention the influence of psycho-pharmaceutical products? How much responsibility can I assume for my actions and feelings? What real chance is there for profound change? I knew these were questions our whole society was struggling with, but I had to understand to what extent those forty years of self-inquiry had indeed influenced my behavior, and if that search had any effect on my personality.

Chapter 19

Moving On

L IKE MANY MEDITATORS I WAS PREVIOUSLY CONVINCED THAT, based on the "awakening to the Truth," with sufficient time, devotion, and training, a happy, kind, and compassionate life was possible no matter a person's life circumstances or personal traits. Together with many other students of various meditation disciplines, I had made a convenient split between this belief and experiencing not so very great results in my personal life. Now I understood that this expectation was an error that came from failing to see that enlightenment—in the sense of non-dual awareness—has no particular bearing on ethics, morals, or a specific kind of behavior.

One of the best examples I found of this misunderstanding was the upheaval caused by some writings by Yasutani *roshi* (1885–1973), a revered and influential figure in the Zen tradition. An article, which appeared in an issue of the Buddhist magazine *Tricycle*, showed that Yasutani clearly expressed anti-Semitic opinions, advocated Japanese participation in World War II, and promoted a fervent nationalism, including Japanese dominance over Asia.[47] In their reaction, stated in the same issue, other Zen teachers provided explanations and excuses why an "enlightened" teacher would behave like this, or else they would redefine enlightenment in various ways. They would acknowledge the influence of upbringing and culture, arguing that morality and justice were dependent upon time and society, but leave the dharma—the Buddhist ethics—unchallenged, seen as ultimate wisdom, and not considered man-made.[48]

My skepticism about the ethical component of non-dual awareness does not affect my admiration for teachers like Bernie Glassman or Tich Nhat Hanh, and others who are activists for peace and the environment. Also, I do not question the immense benefit many people gain through the personality and wisdom of the Dalai Lama and many other teachers. However, anyone would have to be intentionally blind to overlook the many people whose efforts and influence are equally important for world peace, human rights, and the environment—people who are not enlightened or have no background in meditation. I take issue not with specific moral standpoints or deeds, but with the claim that responding to a situation in a specific way is a manifestation of enlightenment and comes out of "this intelligent, wise and timeless presence,"[49] the result of "awakening" to an "unfathomable intelligence—appropriate in each moment...not drawn from memory."[50]

Who would deny that meditative inquiry is a superb tool for learning about ourselves and keeping in perspective our emotions, as well as to observe the consequences of an unchecked self-image, of blinding prejudgments, or other equally destructive thought patterns, through suggestions given by mature and experienced teachers? However, equating the quality of behavior and insight with a specific degree of enlightenment only causes confusion.

My training in Zen had certainly made me more focused in my actions and I had tried to be patient and compassionate. Later, the ongoing attention to the emotional component of my thoughts and deeds had helped me to balance my temper and other difficult aspects of my personality. I had learned to give a voice to my body's subtle messages and become conscious of and face the feelings this attention evokes. Nevertheless, now I became quite certain that my ability to access non-dual awareness, which I originally claimed had brought about this change in my behavior and feelings, was of great support but not the cause of it. The changes were a result of my experiences and the ethical input that I had encountered first at the Zen Center and then through other teachings. By sitting quietly, paying non-judgmental attention to my meandering mind, I had learned to uncover and question what was unconsciously expressed through my individual and cultural upbringing. I had become aware of hidden motives that often determined my actions and speech allowing me to reassess my behavior and to observe whether my conscious convictions were really mirrored in my actions. These psychological changes were made easier and perhaps more effective by my ability to create an emotional "distance" through shifting into non-dual awareness. Yet, I had to accept the limitation of the results of my meditation practice, even after forty years of meditating.

When I turned sixty-five, I retired from my teaching position. I could now move to New York and would, finally, be able to live again with my husband. But I hated New York, with its fast pace and unceasing noise, and I adored my apartment in Vienna. I loved the landscape and especially the vineyards surrounding the city, the many cafés, the lifestyle, my friends. Why did I move? I did not even ask the question. I pushed it to one side. I ignored the heaviness that crawled into my guts, the moments of despair when looking at the mulberry tree outside my bedroom window, the intensity with which my eyes clutched the facades of the old buildings or the far-away silhouette of the hills to the east. I concentrated on deciding what to take with me to New York—books, boxes with postcards, papers, photos, theater programs....how much are you what you have? Several friends questioned how we would fare after being separated for such a long time. Would we be able to learn to live together again? I ignored it all. I could simply not imagine a life without Bob and he was still working in New York. How long could I wait? I felt the pressure of getting older and perhaps sick. If I didn't move now, then perhaps we would never live together again. Yet, though this move and its consequences proved to be the most demanding test ever on our relationship, most of all it brought me to a profound understanding of what it is that lives, has hopes, has relationships, and most of all, has emotions in abundance. This was not something to question in a meditative way. I could easily acquire a completely detached attitude by switching into non-dual awareness. What became crystal clear was that living inevitably meant that I was nothing if not for the memories, whether they were conscious, subconscious, or unconscious. As much as I had known this before, now I knew it in every cell of my body through my forced departure from a life that I had not even known was so much part of who I was.

After my arrival in New York and the initial shock of being exposed to a very different life, I slowly and tentatively adjusted to a free daily schedule, to finding voice students, walks in Central Park, and most of all to be able to hug my husband whenever I felt like it, or almost. But what happened very frequently then, and still sometimes does, I could never have anticipated: I was besieged with flashes of images of Vienna rushing past my inner eye, catching me in the middle of seemingly unrelated moments—in the kitchen preparing food, walking in the park, talking with people, anything. Suddenly, I would see before me street corners of Vienna, parks, meadows, buildings, shops, the Danube, streetcars, each time accompanied by a cutting ache in my stomach or somewhere else in my body. Sometimes the pain was so strong I almost toppled over. Sometimes tears would stream and I couldn't help wailing and sobbing. I couldn't avoid this, but I could prevent myself being lost in these reactions by not permitting incessant repetitions of these images and their accompanying emotional reinforcement once they were conscious. I took to my old refuge of fast walking and switching into a non-dual state of mind. Peace and calm almost instantly replaced the inner turmoil and stayed for a little while. This was still always a wonder which I felt grateful for, but it took several years for the force of the emotional assaults to subside.

Another unexpected encounter with a similar subject also happened a few weeks after I had moved to New York—unexpected, at least in its force. Our internet connection broke down, and I was completely caught by surprise when I realized how devastated I was by not being able to contact my friends in Vienna; I had set up a hidden lifeline of which I had not even been fully aware. I slowly realized how immigrants must feel when they have to face a life in which their whole personal history is barely acknowledged within the setting and the society where they are living. I had to admit to myself that, in spite of my ability to reside in a present that was not tethered to emotional upheavals, I was still living within the boundaries of my biological and psychological needs, and that being an appreciated member of a network was part of those needs.

Although I don't sit formally in meditation very often, having learned to be alert to the inter-relatedness of thought and emotion and to observe closely the consequences of how and what I think, I am managing myself with greater intelligence and opening my attention and concern to a broader environment. There is also often a lightness, a gentle lifting of self-importance. I believe this is a result of the many moments of being nobody. Yet, to my surprise, I have finally discovered that it may not only be acceptable but actually necessary as a human being to have basic psychological needs, such as acknowledgment, respect, purpose, and even an identity. This was a revelation to my mind, which had been fixed on the Buddhist idea that somehow one could live an "unattached" life.

How can I see myself as a specific person with somewhat fixed features, when I also have the experience of being nobody? It is very simple. There is no contradiction when I realize that what I just wrote—having no self, no "I," no body—is only the conceptualization of a body-brain state, something that comes and goes like everything else. Neither seems more "true" or valid. What could be false in sleeping or being awake?

My friend Andrea once stated with a sigh, "Why do we enjoy so much to be understood?" And I also remember screaming at my husband once, "I don't want you to respect my limits! I want you to understand them!" I believe it is this need to be understood and to understand that helps maintain our reality. Going insane often means that we can no longer share with anyone the experiences and emotions that we construct from whatever input we receive. We become isolated and sometimes even lose the "reality" of who we are. I feel intensely how fragile my "world" is, how interwoven with my beliefs and how utterly dependent I am on being connected. Or as one writer notes at the conclusion of the account of her own journey: "We order our memories and link them together, and those disparate fragments gain an owner: the 'I' of autobiography, who is no one without a 'you.'"[51] Those words ring true and bring surprising comfort to this owner, this "I," even if this seems a modest conclusion to arrive at after forty years of questioning and searching.

Afterword

WHAT WAS THE MOST IMPORTANT DISCOVERY OF THIS journey—what was the understanding that I came away with? It was the realization that we always become aware of an experience according to a description, an explanation or a label, and therefore respond to the description and not to the immediate experience. And this includes the experience of enlightenment. Our language and our concepts determine and shape what we believe to be direct experience. As long as we are unaware of this tendency, this trait of our human brain, we will consider our interpretation of what "we have experienced" as an unshakeable truth and we will cling to and fight for this "reality," especially if it is a culturally shared belief or tradition.

I also think I have finally understood that every act, every decision however small, excludes another possibility we could have pursued, another path we could have followed. How can I know what kind of person I would have been without meditation but with other experiences? We live amidst a nexus of consequences that may or may not coincide with our expectations. The gift of stepping out of this network for a while through non-dual awareness into a world free of expectation and consequences is special, important, and wonderful. However, it still leaves me, as a complex and puzzling human animal, determined by the physical boundaries of my brain and my environment, to carry on as best I can.

Glossary

dualistic: generally denotes a view in which the human mind is split into a non-substantial, spiritual part and the substantial, biological part. A related, less common meaning, which is more important in this book, denotes the division into subject and object or I and other, in particular when the separation is dissolved in **non-dual awareness**.

dharma: Buddhist teachings.

koan: a short dialogue, usually between a master and student, used as a teaching tool in some Zen sects. Their core meaning has to be understood and demonstrated to the teacher in the light of non-dual awareness, or *kensho*.

***kensho*:** the term used in Zen for the experience of non-dual awareness, or enlightenment. (from Japanese, "seeing into one's own nature").

***kyosaku*:** a flat wooden stick used by some Zen sects to heighten attention.

Mumonkan: *The Gateless Barrier*, a compilation of Zen koans and commentaries, made in China in the early thirteenth century. Together with the **Hekiganroku**, *The Blue Cliff Record*, compiled in the early twelfth century, it is the best-known collection of koans.

non-dual awareness: a type of consciousness that does not feature subject-object based perception.

rakusu: A hand-sewn rectangular patchwork vestment hung around the neck, symbolizing the patchwork robes worn by the Buddha and his disciples.

roshi: the teacher who guides and inspires Zen training after many years of study and after gaining permission of his or her former teacher to teach.

sangha: community of people practicing Buddhism together.

sesshin: days or weeks of intense *zazen* practice in silence.

zazen: the specific meditation practice of Zen. Emphasis is on quieting the mind and awakening to the Buddha's "ultimate truth." A form of concentrated quiet walking is also considered *zazen*.

zendo: a chamber or hall where *zazen* takes place.

Notes

1 Philip Kapleau, *The Three Pillars of Zen* (1965; New York: Anchor Books, 2000), 14.

2 Even later, I realized that terms such as "sub" were intrinsic to the formidable hierarchism that was, and still is, part of Zen attitude.

3 In Sanskrit, *Prajnaparamita Hrdaya Sutra*.

4 Studying scriptures, expositions, and sermons of the Buddha is not an element of most types of Zen training. One of the arguments for this was the notion that enlightenment is not communicable by words. Another was the well-established fact that the Buddha did not leave any written record of his teachings; the first Buddhist texts date from at least a hundred years after his death.

5 *Hekiganroku* (*The Blue Cliff Record*) was compiled in China in the early twelfth century and *Mumonkan* (*The Gateless Barrier*) in the early thirteenth century.

6 Kapleau, *The Three Pillars of Zen*, 342.

7 Toni Packer died August 23, 2013, in the presence of friends, at the Livingston County Center for Nursing in Mt. Morris, New York.

8 Toni Packer, *The Light of Discovery* (North Clarendon, VT: Charles E. Tuttle Company, 1995), 98.

9   Mihaly Csikszentmilhayi, *Creativity: Flow and the Psychology of Discovery and Invention* (New York: Harper Perennial, 1997).

10   Advaita—*a-* (non-) *dvaita* (dual)—Vedanta originated in Hindu philosophy and is based on the scriptures of the Upanishads, Bhagavad Gita, and the Brahma Sutras. The belief in the interconnectedness of all manifestations is very compatible with Buddhist philosophy, which was also of some influence. Today most teachings of this tradition in the West omit the study of scriptures and rely solely on the experience and understanding of a non-dual awareness as pure Consciousness or the absolute Self. The teacher or guru is seen as a necessity for the pupil to awaken to this state of consciousness. The most influential modern teachers were Ramana Maharshi, H. W. L. Poonja, and Nisargadatta. Many of today's well-known teachers, even those without obvious connections to Advaita Vedanta, were students either of these three gurus or of students of theirs.

11   Nisargadatta, *I Am That* (Durham, NC: Acorn, 1994), 9.

12   Suzanne Segal, *Collision with the Infinite* (San Diego: Blue Dove, 1998).

13   Almaas was the founder of the Ridhwan School, a Sufi-based spiritual teaching approach with the Enneagram as its personality model, an approach that was originally developed by Oscar Ichazo. The Enneagram is a model of possible developments and interrelations of the human psyche and part of a tradition that started with Gurdjieff, but it probably ultimately derives from Sufi or Dervish traditions.

14   A. H. Almaas, *Luminous Night's Journey* (Berkeley: Diamond Books, 1995).

15   The notion of attributing wisdom to non-dual awareness is stated quite forcefully in many interviews with spiritual teachers in *WIE–What Is Enlightenment* 14, Fall/Winter 1998.

16   The main principles of Buddhism focus on the idea that all phenomena are impermanent and constantly changing, that they are interdependent and that they are without any intrinsic identity including the notion of being a separate "me"—needless to say that the confrontation with these

statements is at the center of my elaborations in this book and in my life. Yet the struggle to put these pronouncements into the context of a body-brain equipped with perception and computing that result at the impression of being an individual person has been going on since they were put into the world, not least because nobody can deny that our normal sense of reality is not only helpful for survival but also necessary, no matter how much it may make us suffer according to Buddhist doctrine or how scientifically (in)valid it may be.

17 Ramesh S. Balsekar, in ed. Wayne Liquorman, *Consciousness Speaks* (Redondo Beach, Cal.: Advaita Press, 1992), 17, 18.

18 Eckhart Tolle, *The Power of Now* (Novato, Cal.: New World Library, 1999), 61.

19 Ibid., 164–65.

20 Ibid., 142.

21 J. Krishnamurti, *The Awakening of Intelligence* (New York: Avon Books, 1975) 333.

22 D. Bohm, *Thought as a System* (London & New York: Routledge, 1994).

23 Ibid., 127.

24 R. Maharshi, *The Spiritual Teaching of Ramana Maharshi* (Boston & London: Shambala, 1988).

25 Gangaji, *You Are That!* 2 vols. (Boulder, Colo.: Gangaji Foundation, 1996), 2: 85–86.

26 Jack Kornfield, *After the Ecstasy the Laundry* (New York: Bantam, 2001), 140.

27 Although the latest research on infant moral judgment seems to show a rudimentary sense of "moral thought, moral judgment and moral feeling" (Paul Bloom, "The Moral Lives of Babies," *New York Times*, May 5, 2010)

this certainly does not mean that socialization of these existing tendencies is not influential and necessary.

28 There seems to be a large region of the brain that is active in a kind of "default" or resting state, a network that gets disrupted when a task requiring externally directed attention is performed. Sometimes these networks are referred to as intrinsic and extrinsic. These findings have stirred several kinds of interpretation and seem of importance as an integrating factor in neuro-psychoanalytic theories (Maggie Zellner) and in meditation research (Zoran Josipovic). These concepts appeared earlier in a paper by M. D. Fox, A. Z. Snyder, J. L. Vincent, M. Corbetta, D. C. Van Essen, and M. E. Raichle, "The human brain is intrinsically organized into dynamic, anticorrelated functional networks," *Proceedings of the National Academy of Sciences* 102 (205), 9673–78.

29 He spoke of his neurological experiments with *aplysia californica*, a sea slug, studying its motor integration. He went on to discuss the emerging paradigm of the "embodied mind" to which his research was contributing. The basic premise of the concept of the embodied mind is that perception and action are one; what we perceive is not separable from what we do. In the early nineties the traditional understanding, then still widely accepted, was that a smell, a sound, etc. is perceived through its specific organs and then processed in the brain through a linear hierarchy towards a representation of the environment. Instead, he compared the new view of cell assemblies, firing forward and backward all over the brain, to a bowl of spaghetti. His explanations made me understand that the world in itself has no information; it is only through our motion and acting that we perceive what seems so indisputably the world around us.

30 Francisco Varela, Evan Thompson, Eleanor Rosch, *The Embodied Mind: Cognitive Science and Human Experience* (Cambridge, Mass.: MIT Press, 1995).

31 By the end of the last century, regular meetings had started between the Dalai Lama and western scientists discussing the relationship of Buddhist philosophy to scientific cognitive studies. This resulted in the founding of the Mind and Life Institute (www.mindandlife.org).

32   In 2003 and 2004 test results measuring brain functions during meditation were published for the first time concerning research at the Keck Laboratories at the University of Wisconsin-Madison. The articles appeared in highly regarded scientific journals and were widely noted in the print media. In the first paper, the research team led by the psychologist Richard Davidson had put employees of a biotech firm through a short program in mindfulness-based stress relaxation (MBSR), a standardized form of mindfulness meditation, and reported positive effects on their immune system, which did not show in the control group. The meditators also showed increased activity in the left prefrontal cortex, which had been established by previous research to be associated with a sanguine mental attitude. The second study under Antoine Lutz, working with experienced Buddhist monks, found the appearance of a global (involving the whole brain) "synchrony of gamma waves" which had never been seen to this extent in trial subjects before and was measurable before and after the specific meditation task. This did prove that long-term training in meditation did indeed alter brain structure and functioning. (Part of the goal of a study like this was to see if mental training had lasting effects on brain cells.) Some commentaries connected this global synchronization of brain-cell activity to a unity of perception: an abolition of subject-object differentiation, the feeling of "oneness."

33 James Austin, *Zen and the Brain* (Cambridge, Mass.: MIT Press, 2001).

34 Ibid., 537, 538.

35 Ibid., 66.

36   G. M. Edelman, *Wider Than the Sky: The Phenomenal Gift of Consciousness* (New Haven: Yale University Press, 2004). Although this small volume represents a condensed account of the main conclusions of his studies, on page 9 he gives a concise description of what he means by "remembered present": "Primary consciousness is the state of being mentally aware of things in the world, of having mental images in the present.... Primary consciousness is not accompanied by any sense of a socially defined self with a concept of past or future. It exists primarily in the remembered present." As beings with primary consciousness, we seem to have basic expectations, which include built-in presumptions about

form and space. We also constantly evaluate the outcome of our actions. We—and every other animal—do this, and without it we would not survive very long.

37 Antonio R. Damasio, *The Feeling of What Happens: Body and Emotion in the Making of Consciousness*, (San Diego: Harcourt, 1999), 321; *Descartes' Error: Emotion, Reason and the Human Brain* (New York: Avon Books, 1994) 235.

38 Thomas Metzinger, *Being No One: The Self-Model Theory of Subjectivity* (Cambridge, Mass.: MIT, 2003).

39 As William James, who never seemed at a loss for an insightful comment, noted: "reality 'independent' of human thinking…is a thing very hard to find." In James's view, what we perceive as experience "is always some substitute for it which previous human thinking has…cooked for our consumption." W. James, *Pragmatism: A New Name for Some Old Ways of Thinking. Popular Lectures on Philosophy* (New York: Longmans, Green, 1907), 248, 249.

40 One of the most enlightening books was Susan Blackmore, *Consciousness: An Introduction* (Oxford: Oxford Universtiy Press, 2004). Most beneficial for me were the many surveys and discussions of different philosophical and scientific viewpoints I had never thought of. Most of these discussions centered on the problem which D. Chalmers put forward as "the hard problem": How can a biological explanation be the same as something I individually experience? Along with it went the other hotly discussed issue, which Nagel pinpointed as the subjectivity of our feelings or, as it widely came to be known, as the problem of "qualia," which addressed our personal perception of the world. I am sure that further developments in consciousness research will provide a viable explanation for these seemingly irreconcilable positions.

41 Varela, Thompson, Rosch, *The Embodied Mind*, 169.

42 Blakemore and Cooper performed an experiment in 1970, in which, when kittens were deprived of exposure to vertical lines at a certain sensitive time of their development, they could not later orient themselves in space

(see, for example, E. Bruce Goldstein, *Cognitive Psychology: Connecting Mind, Research and Everyday Experience* [Belmont, Cal.: Wadsworth, 2010], 68). Also, my friend Kevin, who lived in Swaziland, once told me about children who were not able to draw a square, even when shown how to, because no right angle was found in their daily environment. They simply couldn't comprehend it. Similarly, many Austrians cannot differentiate the sound of P or B, because it doesn't exist in their pronunciation of German.

43 S. Pauen, "Denken vor dem Sprechen" (*Gehirn & Geist* 1, 2003). M. Talbot, "The Baby Lab" (*The New Yorker*, September 4, 2006). The report gives an overview of Elizabeth Spelke's research with babies and toddlers based on her premise that "babies come into the world mentally equipped with certain basic systems for ordering it." P. Bloom, *Descartes' Baby* (New York: Basic Books, 2005).

44 "If you don't manipulate the world, you see nothing. When you stop manipulating some aspect of the world, it drops back into nothingness." Susan Blackmore cites Kevin O'Regan and Alva Noë's sensorimotor theory of vision and visual consciousness (2001) and a study by Karn and Hayhoe (2000) which "confirms that spatial information required to control eye movement is retained across saccades" (*Consciousness: An Introduction*, 100–1).

45 The chief premise of constructivism is that the world, myself, and every possible thought I have is created by my genetically driven abilities to categorize and make sense of my environment, and this conceptual understanding is confirmed, denied, varied, and shaped by a constant process of sharing and validating within a complex social and emotional constellation. See: F. B. Simon, *Einführung in Systemtheorie und Konstruktivismus* (Heidelberg: Carl-Auer, 2007); Ernst von Glasersfeld, *Radical Constructivism: A Way of Knowing and Learning* (London: Falmer Press, 1991) and German translation, *Radikaler Konstruktivismus* (Frankfurt: Suhrkamp, 1997); Humberto R. Maturana and Bernhard Poerksen, *Vom Sein zum Tun* (Heidelberg: Carl-Auer, 2002) and English translation, *From Being to Doing* (Heidelberg: Carl-Auer, 2004); Gerhard Roth, *Aus der Sicht des Gehirns* (Frankfurt: Suhrkamp, 2009) 86–89, 230–31.

46   The term "illusion," as used in Buddhist philosophy (and in Hindu philosophy) refers to a concept of not existing, in opposition to the term Truth or Ultimate Reality as existing. If used in constructivism, illusion only opposes a reality that is seen as a more viable concept based on an explanatory model addressing specific circumstances and allowing proof within this context.

47   Brian D. Victoria, "Yasutani Roshi: The Hardest Koan," *Tricycle: The Buddhist Review* (Fall 1999) 62–66.

48   Ibid., 60–75.

49   *WIE—What Is Enlightenment* (Spring/Summer 2003), 106 and 105.

50   In an interview in *WIE—What Is Enlightenment* (Fall/Winter 1998), Steven Batchelor attributes to the Buddha statements giving the characteristics of enlightenment as "not laying claim to an experience of some absolute as the defining characteristic of what awakening is, but rather to an interwoven complex of truths that have to do with suffering, the origins of suffering, the ending of suffering and the path that leads to the ending of suffering....a *vision* of a resolution...." (p. 112; my emphasis). Yet he writes in the same article: "The response to experience through, say, insight or awakening may open up to us the depth of reality, and the profound mystery of reality, but not in a way that alienates us from the contingencies and exigencies of the relative, ambiguous world that we inhabit" (p. 110). Roshi Bernie Glassman says, "I look at compassion as the functioning of that empty state" (*WIE—What Is Enlightenment* [Spring/Summer 2001], 73).

51   Siri Hustvedt, *The Shaking Woman or a History of My Nerves* (New York: Picador, 2011), 198.

About the Author

Dagmar Apel began practicing Zen Buddhism in 1970 with Roshi Philip Kapleau at the Rochester Zen Center, and she has since been deeply involved in meditation practice. She studied with Jiddu Krishnamurti and was an assistant, co-teacher, and close friend of the late Toni Packer of the Springwater Center. She originally trained as a classical singer, touring extensively with the a capella group "Collegium Vocale Köln," performing contemporary and Renaissance music. She received her Master's degree in Functional Voice Training from Antioch University in 1990, and is also a certified Feldenkrais practitioner. For more than a decade she was on the faculty of the University of Music and Performing Arts in Vienna. She currently works as a voice coach and lives with her husband in New York.

Made in the USA
San Bernardino, CA
10 November 2016